Clwyd Railways

IN OLD PHOTOGRAPHS

To Danielle, Zoe, Ben, Rebecca,
Harry and Amy

Clwyd Railways

IN OLD PHOTOGRAPHS

Collected by Mike Hitches
and Jim Roberts

Alan Sutton Publishing Limited
Phoenix Mill · Far Thrupp
Stroud · Gloucestershire

First published 1994

Front cover illustration: Train at Mochdre and
Pabo

Copyright © 1994 Mike Hitches and Jim
Roberts

British Library Cataloguing in Publication Data

A catalogue record for this book is available
from the British Library

ISBN 0 7509 0684 7

Typeset in 9/10 Sabon.
Typsetting and origination by
Alan Sutton Publishing Limited.
Printed and bound by
Redwood Books, Trowbridge, Wiltshire

Contents

Introduction

The railway system in Clwyd covers the old counties of Flintshire, in the east, and Denbighshire, in the west, both very different in character. They were merged together to form the larger county of Clwyd under local government re-organization in 1974. Eastern Clwyd is very much the industrial centre of north Wales, and, as the old county of Flintshire, the area was littered with coal mines, quarries, steelworks, brickworks and other industries, which led to a high concentration of railways serving the area. Denbighshire, on the other hand, depended much more on the tourist trade as the basis of its economy, which was developed as a result of the construction of the Chester and Holyhead Railway, and railways within the old county were much more sparse, its most important route being along the coast.

Three major railway companies were responsible for operation of trains in Clwyd – the London and North Western Railway, the Great Western Railway and the Great Central Railway. These became the London, Midland and Scottish Railway, the GWR and the London and North Eastern Railway following the 1923 Grouping. As far as the Clwyd coast was concerned, the LNWR/LMS held a monopoly of traffic, as owners of the Chester and Holyhead Railway, while industrial east Clwyd was shared between the GWR and GCR/LNER, although the LNWR and Cambrian Railways operated some services into Wrexham.

With three different companies operating trains within the county, there was a wide variety of locomotives to be seen heading passenger and freight trains, from small tank engines on local passenger and freight services, to large express locos on important trains operated by the LNWR/LMS and GWR. In between, there were all manner of locos on secondary passenger and long-distance freight trains. To keep these trains running, locosheds and servicing facilities were provided by the railway companies and, where there are photographs of sheds included in the following pages, sample allocations are noted to give some idea of the variety of motive power that could be seen in the county.

Just as important were the railway stations in the county, from the largest, serving major destinations on the railway timetable, to local halts, which often saw infrequent services handling all too few passengers. Differences in the architectural styles adopted by the railway companies are reflected in the photographs, and give each route its own distinct character.

From the opening of the Shrewbury and Chester Railway, which was to eventually become part of the GWR Paddington–Birkenhead route, in 1846, and the Chester and Holyhead Railway in 1848, the railway network in Clwyd expanded rapidly, particularly in the east of the county, where the complex of lines into Wrexham was fully established by the turn of the century, covering most areas of population in the county. Strangely, however, no branches were built west of Rhyl until the Chester and Holyhead line reached Llandudno Junction in Caernarvonshire, which is outside the scope of this book.

As the nineteenth century drew to a close, the railways serving Clwyd were complete, and went on to handle all required traffic for well over half a century, until Dr Beeching's Reshaping Report of 1963 brought about the closure of many of the lines and stations within the county, and the rationalization of others. There had been closure to passengers of some routes in the years prior to the Beeching Report, but the majority of these lines had remained open for freight traffic until the Beeching 'axe' fell on them. Nowadays, the only line with regular express trains running over it is the Chester and Holyhead route, although many of its stations have ceased to exist. Its importance as the premier line for Ireland, and for the seaside tourist trade, has ensured its future. The other main line, that of the GWR's Paddington–Birkenhead route, has been downgraded to a local line, and that only going as far as Wolverhampton. Wrexham is still on the railway map, but only served by local passenger services to Chester and the Wirral. No freight trains run through the town, the lorry now handling this traffic. Thus, the heyday of the railways in Clwyd is but a memory.

In preparing this volume, I hope that I have, in some way, recalled the time when the railway was the most important means of transport in Clwyd, and its presence in the landscape seemed as permanent as the hills that are part of the county.

SECTION ONE

The Chester and Holyhead Railway

Opened in 1848 by the Chester and Holyhead Railway Company, this main line was constructed as part of a link between London (Euston) and the Irish Sea packet port of Holyhead, on Anglesey, for boat connections to Dublin, Never financially sound, the CHR was absorbed into the London and North Western Railway empire in 1859. Its most famous train was the 'Irish Mail' which, in the summer months, ran twice daily each way, one in the day and one at night. During the winter, only a night train operated. Over the years, this very special train was hauled by most top-link express locomotives of the LNWR. It is however best remembered with LMS 4–6–0 'Royal Scot' locos at the head, these being introduced on the service in 1930. Under BR auspices, the 'Irish Mail' became 'Britannia' Pacific-hauled from 1954 until replaced by Class 40 diesel-electric locos in 1960.

Along with its main role of connecting London with Ireland, the route played an important part in the development of the tourist industry in the west of Clwyd. As the line runs along the north Wales coast, the LNWR and, after the 1923 Grouping, the LMS advertised resorts at places like Colwyn Bay, Rhyl and Prestatyn in an effort to attract passengers to the line. So successful were these campaigns that visitors came to the north Wales coast in their thousands, allowing rapid expansion of the resort towns. They came on summer excursion trains and scheduled expresses from places like Manchester, Liverpool and Birmingham, these trains being hauled by a wide variety of locos of the LNWR, LMS, and BR. To cater for local traffic calling at all stations along the line, tank locos and small tender engines headed non-corridor coaching stock.

The CHR main line was also important for transit of freight, serving quarries at Llandulas and the now threatened coal mine at Point of Air, along with the docks at Mostyn. To sort the substantial quantities of freight traffic operating along the line, both generated within the county and from Caernarvonshire to the west, along with freight to and from Ireland, a major marshalling yard was established at Mold Junction.

Today the Chester and Holyhead main line is still very much in existence, attracting a great deal of traffic during the summer months. Much of the system has, however, been rationalized since the 1960s, and many stations in Clwyd have been closed as a result of Dr Beeching's Reshaping Report of 1963.

Mold Junction locoshed in the mid-1950s with its typical allocation of freight and mixed-traffic locomotives. The shed was responsible for supplying locos for goods traffic emanating from the nearby Mold Junction marshalling yard where much traffic from north Wales, including slate trains from Snowdonia quarries, was sorted in its nine hundred wagon-capacity sidings. The eight-road locoshed had an allocation of locos suited to its role, as indicated in this sample for January 1960. At this time it was coded 6B.

Ex-LMS Stanier 2–6–0	42945, 42965, 42967, 42971, 42973, 42976, 42981, 42982.
Ex-LMS 4F 0–6–0	44065, 44445, 44493.
Ex-LMS Stanier 'Black 5' 4–6–0	44800, 44917, 44935, 45028, 45031, 45042, 45043, 45055, 45070, 45072, 45225, 45247, 45275, 45325, 45345.
Ex-LMS 'Patriot' class 4–6–0	45501 *St Dunstans**
	45511 *Isle of Man**
	45546 *Fleetwood**
	45548 *Lytham St Annes**
Ex-LMS 'Jinty' 0–6–0T	47269, 47615, 47646, 47650.
Ex-LMS 8F 2–8–0	48054, 48074, 48166, 48175, 48246, 48259, 48264, 48323, 48458, 48697, 48749, 48753, 48754, 48771.
Ex-WD 2–8–0	90147, 90187, 90227, 90532, 90566, 90606, 90702.

* The 'Patriot' class 4–6–0s only stayed at Mold Junction for four months, and were the only named locos to be allocated to the shed.

LMS 4F 0–6–0 No. 4375 outside Mold Junction shed on 6 July 1935, an example of the type of loco used on freight work at the nearby marshalling yard. These, along with 'Black 5s' and 8Fs, were the mainstay of the shed. The marshalling yard was closed in May 1964, with the locoshed being shut on 18 April 1966, its last allocation being ten 'Black 5s' thirteen 8Fs and one 0–6–0 'Jinty' tank, No. 47598.

LMS 'Black 5' 4–6–0 No. 5110 at Mold Junction shed on 6 July 1935. This loco stayed in North Wales for most of its life, retiring into preservation from Holyhead shed in March 1964. The engine is now based on the Severn Valley Railway at Bridgnorth as No. 45110 and is named *RAF Biggin Hill*.

Sandycroft station looking towards Chester shortly before closure in 1966. A station was first opened at Sandycroft on 1 March 1884, a basic two-sleeper platformed structure with small wooden shelters and cast-iron foot-bridge. It stood on the Queensferry side of a level crossing and remained in existence until the Chester and Holyhead line was quadrupled as far as Llandudno Junction in 1900 when a new, much-enlarged station was opened at Sandycroft. A road overbridge replaced the original level crossing and, on 1 June 1899, longer platforms were provided on the outer slow lines, and standard LNWR wooden buildings were placed on the platforms. However, a brick-built booking office was provided at road level. From the booking office, a long foot-bridge connected the platforms. The LNWR also provided a timber-and brick-built signal-box, which was built between the main Up and Down lines, opposite the platforms, and a row of employees' cottages were situated behind the Up (to Chester) platform. Less than a mile west of Sandycroft station were Dundas Sidings, serving the coal mines of Admiral Dundas. These were greatly increased in size during the 1900 track-widening scheme and became important in the First World War as munitions production in the area expanded.

On a semi-fast train at Shotton (Low Level) is an ex-Midland Railway three-cylinder Compound 4–4–0. The train is calling at the station on its way to Chester. Shotton's LNWR station opened on 1 April 1907, and was one of the last to be built on the Chester and Holyhead line, being placed immediately west of an intersection bridge carrying the ex-Great Central Railway's north Wales to Liverpool line. The station consisted of platforms to the outer slow lines, which were connected by a foot-bridge. The platforms were of brick construction with wooden station buildings, but there was no road access, passengers gaining access via the High Level GCR station. The station closed in 1966 as Chester and Holyhead rationalization took effect, but it was re-opened in 1972 to serve the British Steel (ex-John Summers Ltd) works nearby. CHR rationalization had meant that the old four-track formation had been reduced to two, and timber platforms for the new station were constructed on the old track formation. The timber platforms have since been replaced by concrete. Incidentally, preserved BR 9F 2–10–0 No. 92203, now named *Black Prince*, was working at the local steelworks when it was withdrawn from service in 1967. She now operates on the East Somerset Railway and is owned by the artist David Shepherd. Around 1937 there was a major strike at Shotton steelworks, and the management brought in blackleg labour from along the coast. In an attempt to deter these people from going to work, the strikers lined the track, near the station, and stoned trains bringing the blacklegs to the works. Even the station-master was pelted as he closed the train doors. Eventually, police were drafted in to quell the trouble.

The two-platformed Connah's Quay station opened on 25 May 1906, replacing the original opened on 1 September 1870. The new station had brick buildings which were designed by CHR architect Francis Thompson. Connah's Quay itself was developed by the Wrexham, Mold and Connah's Quay Railway Company, later to become part of the Great Central Railway, and became a customer of the LNWR with the opening of Connah's Quay station. Just west of the station a branch curved away to Connah's Quay, which was controlled by Connah's Quay No. 2 signal-box. The station closed to passengers in 1966 and was soon demolished.

In the background, the cooling towers of Rockliffe Hall power station can be seen, with its own sidings to supply the power station with coal from local collieries. From Connah's Quay to Bagillt, the four-track formation was reduced to two tracks. The power station, sadly, no longer exists, its cooling towers having been demolished in recent years. From the power station the line passes through a wooded cutting and then through the 98 yd Rockliffe Tunnel on its way to Flint.

Entering Connah's Quay station is the 2.45 p.m. express from Llandudno to Birmingham (New Street) on Sunday 4 August 1957. The train is being hauled by 'Black Five' 4–6–0 No. 45448 of Aston shed, Birmingham (3D). The loco had probably brought a train down from Birmingham the previous day and had been stabled and serviced overnight at Llandudno Junction before returning the following day. The cooling towers of Rockliffe Hall power station can be clearly seen on the right of the picture, as can the lattice-girder station foot-bridge.

Flint station (now spelt Fflint, the new spelling influenced by the recent revival of the Welsh language, which would pronounce the single 'F' spelling as Vlint, the extra 'F' softening to an 'F' pronunciation) looking towards the west. On entering the station from Chester the remains of the Plantagenet castle, once on the bank of the River Dee, can be seen to the right. During the last century Flint was a very busy port and in the 1880s it supplied Muspratt's chemical works, which in those days was the largest employer in the area. The works can be seen just beyond the station foot-bridge, having become part of the Courtalds Group by this time. Like many of the old industries in the area, the works no longer exists. In 1979 Flint station acquired park-and-ride facilities and had its Down platform extended.

Caprotti valve-geared ex-LMS 'Black Five' 4–6–0 No. 44741 of Llandudno Junction shed (6G) is seen passing Flint station with a Llandudno-bound train. These locos were a rather unusual version of this ubiquitous class of 4–6–0s, although Llandudno Junction shed had a few of them and they were a fairly common sight on the north Wales coast. The unusual steampipe arrangement to the cylinders, however, did nothing to help the appearance of what, in standard form, was a very attractive locomotive.

Flint station looking towards Chester, showing the station foot-bridge in the distance and a bridge in the foreground which provided a public right of way over the railway. The station buildings were designed by Francis Thompson in 1848, when the station opened, and they are retained to the present day. The goods shed, just visible on the left behind the main station building, was erected in 1860. Just beyond Flint the line was quadrupled to Llandulas, a distance of some 24 miles, between 1896 and 1915 and runs on a virtually straight course past marshland, at the mouth of the Dee. On the right the Wirral can also be seen in the distance.

On the right of the picture is the signal-box which controlled movements at Flint. It replaced an original CHR example which controlled a level crossing that was once situated here until replaced by the overbridge. Once the overbridge had made the level crossing redundant, the station platforms were extended across the old crossing site. Incidentally, the station foot-bridge had originally been located at Sandycroft, and was moved to Flint in 1901.

BR 'Britannia' Pacific No. 70047 is seen at the head of a Down train to Holyhead in the early 1960s. These engines appeared on the Chester and Holyhead line in 1953, when they were introduced as replacements for ex-LMS 'Royal Scot' 4–6–0s on the famous 'Irish Mail' trains which ran nonstop between Holyhead and Euston. More of these locos, including the doyen of the class, No. 70000 *Britannia*, appeared on the north Wales coast, along with ex-LMS 'Princess Coronation' Pacifics, when the West Coast Main Line was modernized in the early 1960s, making them redundant on Scottish expresses. They became the mainstay of express power until replaced by Class 40 diesels in the mid-1960s.

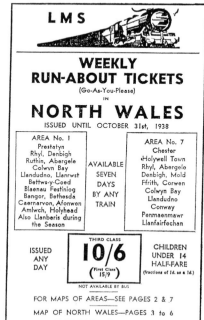

The LMS was keen, in the 1920s and '30s, to generate excursion traffic along the north Wales coast and advertised cheap excursion tickets during the summer months. One such advert showed 'Go-As-You-Please' tickets for 10s. 6d. (52½p) in 1938.

Approaching Flint from the west is an Up train, double-headed by BR 'Standard' class 5 4–6–0 No. 73030 and an unidentified ex-LMS 'Black Five' 4–6–0. In the background is Muspratt's chemical works. The BR class 5s were a development of the famous LMS Stanier-designed 'Black 5s', which had been so successful since their introduction in the mid-1930s, being common all over the old LMS network, including along the north Wales coast.

Bagillt station, some two miles west of Flint, lay in the middle of what was once Bettinsfield Colliery, and was the reason for its existence. The station closed in 1966, and only the rotting remains of the Up platform remind one of its existence.

An LMS advert for spring season excursions to stations on the Chester and Holyhead line in 1925.

An ex-Lancashire and Yorkshire Railway 52xxx Aspinall 0–6–0, probably of Rhyl locoshed, idles away its time at Bagillt station as it waits for a number of trains to pass through, judging by the number of cleared signals. Bagillt station was originally opened in 1849 to cater for a need that existed at that time. It was resited in 1871 to its final location, which also accommodated a small goods yard, capable of holding some 73 wagons, on the Down side of the main line. The station buildings were rather grand when compared to the importance of the station. Freight services at Bagillt ceased on 4 May 1964, but the old goods shed remained and was still being used quite recently. Widening of the railway through Bagillt in 1907 resulted in the addition of two lines on the Up side, and the station being provided with a new Up platform, the one on the Down side being retained. The new station was completed in June 1907 and served until it was closed.

Holywell station's Francis Thompson-designed Italianate-style main station building as it appeared in the mid-1950s. The station was closed in 1966, but the main building was given a preservation order, the first station in north Wales to be so treated. It still exists and is well maintained.

Holywell Junction station, looking towards Chester. The station was opened in 1848 and was given 'Junction' status with the opening of a short branch to Holywell town in 1912.

Ex-LMS 'Black 5' 4–6–0 No. 44769 heads a goods train from Holyhead to Mold Junction through Holywell Junction station on 7 August 1962. The station at Holywell had undergone quite a few changes since opening in 1848, not least when the main line was quadrupled, necessitating two extra platforms. A subway with inclined footways connected all the platforms, so there was no station foot-bridge. New buildings were provided for the newly added platforms, in brick on the island platform and timber on the Up platform, all being of standard LNWR pattern. The station was also provided with substantial goods facilities, complete with a goods shed. Since closure nothing, except the main building, remains of what was once a substantial CHR station.

The western end of Holywell Junction station, showing the island platform and Up platform, along with subway entrances.

The LNWR was very much aware of the tourist potential of the Chester and Holyhead line, given that it served many of the north Wales coast resorts, and advertised its scenic advantages, as shown in this early twentieth-century poster.

Mostyn station looking towards Chester. The station was opened by the CHR in 1848. A goods shed was provided at this end. Goods facilities were also provided on the Up side for the Darwen and Mostyn Iron Company and nearby Mostyn Docks. The docks are still in use today and are being extended to provide facilities for Hamilton Oil work underway just out to sea. However, there have been some problems, with the oil company saying that its land base is to be on Merseyside, after the Secretary of State for Wales asked for a planning inquiry following protests by conservationists, who were concerned about the effects on the birdlife of the Dee Estuary mud flats if oil development were allowed to go ahead. The decision to establish its land base elsewhere has angered locals, who have seen potential job prospects disappear with Hamilton Oil's announcement. The LNWR sidings had capacity for ninety-three wagons.

The main station building at Mostyn, in Francis Thompson's rather grand style. These buildings were erected because Mostyn Estate wanted a 'first-class' station, rather than a Halt, which was really all that was required. The railway in the area was quadrupled, the work being completed on 22 June 1902, and an island platform was added. The station closed to passengers in 1966 and nothing now remains.

Entering Mostyn station is the Sunday's all-stations train from Chester to Llandudno, on 4 August 1957. The train is headed by 'Jubilee' class 4–6–0 No. 45731 *Perseverance* of Chester shed (6A). Motive power for passenger trains along the Chester and Holyhead main line was not usually supplied by locosheds in Clwyd, expresses operating between Holyhead, Euston, the north-west and west midlands being either supplied by home sheds like Manchester Longsight and Liverpool Edge Hill, or Holyhead. Trains between Llandudno and England were provided by locos from Llandudno Junction, Chester, Crewe or home sheds.

On Sunday 4 August 1957, the 12.45 p.m. Sunday service from Holyhead to Euston enters Talacre station headed by BR 'Britannia' Pacific No. 70032 *Tennyson* of Longsight shed, Manchester (9A), with ex-LMS 'Black 5' 4–6–0 No. 45073 of Crewe South shed (5B) as pilot engine. This is a rather unusual mix of motive power for a Holyhead–Euston train, as it would usually have been powered by a loco from Holyhead or Camden. Talacre station was only opened in 1903, after quadrupling of track in the area. Its buildings were of wooden construction and rather basic. Just visible on the far left of the picture are the sidings which held up to forty-four wagons, connected to the Down slow line. The station closed in 1966 and has now disappeared. Talacre marked the end of industrial Clwyd and, as the line curves gently west, the world of the holidaymaker now encroaches as rows of caravans can be seen on each side of the railway right through to the outskirts of Colwyn Bay. This marks the change in the economic structure in the western section of Clwyd, very much a result of the development of the CHR in the last century.

E STATION, PRESTATYN.

Prestatyn station was the first of the holidaymaking destinations from Chester, and appears to be busy in this pre-First World War view. The fashions of the day give a good deal of interest to the picture, with women in heavy long dresses and fancy hats, and even a parasol in evidence. Male headgear consists of the straw boater, which was popular on Edwardian summer days. The train at the island platform appears to be packed with passengers returning home after a day excursion. The line between Prestatyn and Rhyl had been quadrupled by 1901 and the island platform, complete with wooden building and awning, was opened with the widening of the railway, just as Prestatyn was becoming popular with tourists. Thus, the extra facilities were most welcome. To generate extra traffic, the LMS, which had taken over the CHR from the LNWR following the 1923 Grouping, went into partnership with Thomas Cook to develop a holiday camp at Prestatyn. It opened in June 1939, just before the outbreak of the Second World War. Containing nine hundred chalets, a week's holiday cost £3 13s. 6d. (£3.67½). The camp was taken over by the army during the war and never returned to LMS ownership. Pontins operated a holiday centre at Prestatyn in the post-war years.

No. M 1984.

LMS
LONDON MIDLAND AND SCOTTISH RAILWAY
SEASON EXCURSIONS.

EVERY WEEK-DAY (EXCEPT SATURDAYS), June 1 to July 10,
A SPECIAL EXCURSION WITH OBSERVATION CAR
WILL BE RUN FROM

PRESTATYN to LLANBERIS
(For SNOWDON SUMMIT).
With Bookings to intermediate stations as shown.

THIRD CLASS RETURN FARES—TO

FROM	Times of Starting.	Abergele.	Old Colwyn.	Colwyn Bay.	Llandudno Junction.	Conway.	Penmaenmawr.	Llanfairfechan.	Aber.	Bangor.	Menai Bridge.	Carnarvon.	Llanberis.	Snowdon Summit
	a.m.	s. d.	s. d.	s. d.	s. d.	s. d.	s. d.	s. d.	s. d.	s. d.	s. d.	s. d.	s. d.	s. d.
Prestatyn	9 0	1 0	1 7	1 9	2 3	2 5	2 11	3 3	3 7	4 2	4 5	5 3	6 5	12 5
Rhyl	9 10	0 7	1 2	1 4	1 10	1 11	2 6	2 10	3 1	3 9	3 11	4 10	5 11	11 11
Abergele	9 18	—	0 7	0 9	1 3	1 5	1 11	2 3	2 7	3 2	3 2	3 5	5 5	11 5
Old Colwyn	9 28	—	—	0 10	1 5	1 8	2 3	2 9	3 1	3 8	4 10	10 10
Colwyn Bay	9 31	—	—	0 6	0 8	1 3	1 6	1 11	2 2	2 9	3 8	4 8	10 8
Llandudno	9 A 39	—	—	—	1 1	1 5	1 8	2 4	2 6	3 6	4 6	10 6
Deganwy	9 A 36	—	—	—	0 10	1 2	1 5	2 1	2 3	2 4	3 10	3 10 3
Llandudno Junction	9 50	—	—	—	0 9	1 0	1 3	1 11	2 3	0 4	2 10 2
Conway	9 54	—	—	—	0 7	0 11	1 3	1 0	2 11	4 0	10 0
Penmaenmawr	10 5	—	—	—	0 4	0 7	1 3	1 6	2 4	3 5	9 5
Llanfairfechan	10 11	—	—	—	0 3	1 0	1 2	2 0	3 2	9 2
Aber	10 17	—	—	—	0 8	0 10	1 9	2 11	8 11
Bangor	10 35	—	—	—	0 3	1 1	2 2	8 2
Menai Bridge	10 39	—	—	—	0 11	2 0	8 0
Port Dinorwic	10 48	—	—	—	0 6	1 8	7 8
Carnarvon	11 10	—	—	—	1 2	7 2
Llanberis ...... arrive	11 30													

Passengers go forward from Llanberis to Snowdon Summit at 12.0 noon.

A—Passengers change at Llandudno Junction into Special Train.

SNOWDON SUMMIT.—The Snowdon Mountain Tramroad Co. reserve the power to stop the Train from proceeding above a certain height in the event of snow, or should the weather prove otherwise unsuitable for the complete ascent.

Return Arrangements.—Passengers return on day of issue of ticket by the services shown below :—

FROM	Times of Departure.		FROM	Times of Departure.	
	p.m.	p.m.		p.m.	p.m.
SNOWDON SUMMIT	1.30 or 2.30	1.30 or 2.30	Conway	6 39	8 33
Llanberis	5 10	6 50	Llandudno Junction	6 48	8 59
Carnarvon	5 35	7 18	Colwyn Bay	6 55	9 10
Menai Bridge	5 54	7 35	Old Colwyn	7 1	9 17
Bangor	6 5	8 0	Abergele	7 8	9 32
Aber	6 15	8 10	Rhyl	7 28	10 10
Llanfairfechan	6 22	8 16	Prestatyn .... arr.	7 35	10 17
Penmaenmawr	6 28	8 22			

Note.—FOR PARTICULARS OF OBSERVATION CAR SEE OTHER SIDE.

Children under 3 years of age free ; 3 and under 12 half-fares.   No Luggage allowed.

CONDITIONS OF ISSUE OF EXCURSION TICKETS.

EXCURSION TICKETS are NOT transferable and will be available only to and from the stations named upon them, and by the trains, and on the dates specified on the announcements. The Company give notice that tickets for Excursions are issued at a reduced rate, and subject to the condition that the Company shall not be liable for any loss, damage, injury or delay to passengers, arising from any cause whatsoever. Day and Half-day Excursion tickets will not be extended, nor will any allowance be made on return portions not used.

All information regarding Excursion Trains on the London Midland and Scottish Railway be obtained on application to Divisional Passenger Commercial Superintendent, Victoria St Manchester.

May, 1925.   (XM 34615/C)   H. G. BURGESS, General Mana

McCorquodale & Co., Limited, Printers, London—Works, Newton.—890

An LMS excursion timetable for trips from Prestatyn to Llanberis in Snowdonia. The railway company was keen to offer day trips like this as a way of attracting extra revenue on weekdays, especially from holidaymakers who might enjoy an excursion away from their resort.

Three and three-quarter miles west of Prestatyn lies the important station of Rhyl. It is still one of the four big revenue-earners for the railway along the coast. In 1938 750,000 people arrived at Rhyl, 639,000 between May and September. Even today there are always plenty of people waiting to board trains at Rhyl. This early twentieth-century view shows the exterior of Rhyl station with its substantial iron and glass entrance canopy and large station building, which befitted such an important station. This building contained every facility required for such a large station, including waiting and refreshment rooms, as well as all staff offices. The building in this view was an LNWR replacement for an original Francis Thompson structure, which was removed when quadrupling was undertaken at Rhyl.

The main Up platform at Rhyl at the turn of the century. It shows the steel and glass platform canopy and typical LNWR platform notices, along with the W.H. Smith newspaper kiosk (so common on railway stations in those days), the platform side of the main station building, the bay window of the refreshment room, and the covered foot-bridge to the opposite platform. There seems to be a train due, judging by the number of waiting passengers.

In the early 1950s BR introduced a railway circular tour of north Wales, the starting point originally being at Rhyl, which became known as the 'North Wales Land Cruise'. This tour covered many of the branches in Clwyd, going as far as Portmadoc on the Cambrian coast line, and Caernarfon before returning home. This advert dates from 1959.

NORTH WALES
RADIO LAND CRUISE

SPECIALLY EQUIPPED FOR ACTUAL RADIO RECEPTION AND DESCRIPTIVE COMMENTARY ON FEATURES OF INTEREST EN ROUTE.
FOR MAP OF ROUTE PLEASE SEE OVERLEAF.

TUESDAYS and THURSDAYS
7th JULY to 23rd JULY, 1959 (inclusive)
ALSO
MONDAYS to FRIDAYS
27th JULY to 4th SEPTEMBER, 1959 (inclusive)

FARE	Time of departure	FROM	Arrival on Return
s. d.	a.m.		p.m.
	10 10	PWLLHELI	5 C25
	10 18	PENYCHAIN	5 C15
	10 30	CRICCIETH	5 18
	10 42	PORTMADOC	5 26
13/-	10 50	PENRHYNDEUDRAETH	5 37
	10*40	TALSARNAU	5 42
	11 0	HARLECH	5 50
	10*57	LLANBEDR & PENSARN	5 58
FROM	11 12	DYFFRYN ARDUDWY	6 6
EACH STATION	11 15	TALYBONT HALT	6 12
	11 25	BARMOUTH	6 17
	11 45	PENMAENPOOL	7 *36
	11 50	DOLGELLEY	7 *41
	11‡25	BALA	8†*42
	p.m.		
	12 50	CORWEN	9 * 3

RHYL arrive 1-58 p.m.	RHYL depart 3-30 p.m.

*—Change at Barmouth   C—Change at Afon Wen
‡—Change at Bala Junction and Corwen.   †—Change at Bala Junction.

Children under Three years of age, Free; Three and under Fourteen years of age, Half-fare.

LIGHT MEALS AND REFRESHMENTS, MAY BE OBTAINED FROM THE CAFETERIA CAR ON THE TRAIN.

HOLIDAY RUNABOUT TICKETS ARE NOT AVAILABLE BY THIS TRAIN

For conditions of issue of these tickets, also luggage allowances, see the British Transport Commission's Regulations and Conditions of Issue of Tickets, etc.

Further information will be supplied on application to the Stations, or to Mr. O. VELTOM, District Traffic Superintendent. Oswestry (Telephone Oswestry 189, Extn. 211); Mr. W. GRIFFITHS, District Commercial Manager, Shrewsbury (Telephone Shrewsbury 3614, Extn. 65) or to Mr. E. FLAXMAN, Commercial Officer, Paddington Station, W.2.

BRITISH RAILWAYS

An unidentified ex-LMS Stanier 2–6–0 heads a short parcels train along the through lines at Rhyl station in the late 1950s. By this time the station had taken on something of a shabby appearance, compared with the previous picture taken in LNWR days. Things have changed a great deal since the heyday of steam at Rhyl. Beyond the Down platform there were once substantial sidings, but all have now gone, the land being taken over for shop and housing development. The station itself has become rather tatty and neglected-looking, although the main building and platform canopy survive as a reminder of the days when holidaymakers always travelled by train to the resort.

Rhyl was also supplied with a three-road locoshed, which provided motive power for the branch to Denbigh, local freight traffic and shunting duties in the goods yard. This view of the station yard, with a 'Jinty' 0–6–0 tank engine being coaled, shows the sort of locos that were allocated there. Typical allocations were as follows:

January 1960
LMS 3F 0–6–0	43618
LMS 4F 0–6–0	43981, 44367
LMS 3F 0–6–0T	47350
L&Y 3F 0–6–0	52119, 52162, 52438
MR 2F 0–6–0	58287
BR class 2 2–6–0	78031, 78055, 78056

The shed also had an allocation of BR class 4 4–6–0s between 1957 and 1959, and from June 1960 to September 1962. The shed was closed in February 1963, its last allocation being:

LMS 3F 0–6–0	47350, 47507, 47669
BR class 2 2–6–2T	84003

The Up 'Emerald Isle Express', hauled by ex-LMS rebuilt 'Jubilee' class 4–6–0 No. 45522 *Prestatyn* of Camden shed (1B), waits at Abergele and Pensarn station on 15 April 1956. This train operated between Holyhead and Euston, hence the London-based loco at the head, to connect with ferries from Dun Laoghaire, near Dublin. The station in this view dates from 1902, when the lines were widened. An unusual feature is the station name on a stone tablet set into the station wall on the Up side. Another stone station name can be seen at Bangor. The signal-box was set centrally between the Up and Down running lines as part of the quadrupling scheme. Goods facilities were also provided here, and an original wooden goods shed was replaced in LMS days by a concrete structure. In the right background are camping coaches, provided by the railway company to give cheap family holidays and to earn some extra revenue. These coaches were placed in a siding behind the Up platform to give easy access to the beach. From Abergele the line ran close to the seashore all the way to Colwyn Bay.

Ex-LMS 2–6–0 No. 42958 runs through Abergele and Pensarn station with a fitted-freight train in August 1963. To the right, on the Down platform, is the original Thompson station building, which survived track widening and still exists today.

An LMS advert for conducted tours of north Wales on weekdays.

THE JETTIES LLANDDULAS.

COPYRIGHT

The jetties and railway sidings serving a limestone quarry at Llandulas. Railway wagons containing stone products are visible in this view. Between here and Abergele, the worst accident ever to occur on the CHR took place in August 1868, and resulted in the loss of thirty-seven lives. On 20 August a pick-up goods train arrived at Llandulas sidings at 12.24 p.m. with forty-three wagons, two of which contained paraffin casks collected at Saltney. Unfortunately, all of the goods train could not be accommodated in the sidings, but by dividing the train there was room for it to shunt clear. While a shunting operation was being prepared, the Down 'Irish Mail' was due to pass through. Rules stated that all shunting on the main line had to be completed at least ten minutes before a train was due. In breach of these rules, the Llandulas station-master insisted that shunting be carried out. While shunting was carried out, the rear six wagons were left on the main line on a gradient of 1 in 147 and 1 in 100 falling towards Abergele. None of the wagon brakes were pinned down, except that on the brake van. Three timber wagons were drawn out of the siding and fly-shunted back on to the standing vehicles, with the brakesman running beside and attempting to apply the brakes. He failed and they hit the wagons on the main line, causing the brake cog on the brake van to fracture and all the wagons, which included those carrying paraffin, to run away. At 12.39 the 'Irish Mail' ran through Abergele some five minutes late. Only 1¾ miles west of Abergele, the driver saw the runaway wagons approaching. When he realized what was happening the wagons were almost upon the train. The driver jumped, but the fireman, who was trying to apply the brakes, did not escape. On impact, the front of the 'Irish Mail' was engulfed in paraffin. Spilt coal from the loco's firebox caused it to ignite, and the fire consumed the first four coaches, all of which were locked. The fireman and thirty-six passengers were killed. The fire was so intense that only two of the victims could be identified. The inquiry that followed blamed the LNWR for the accident, stating many rules had been ignored. The victims of the accident now lie in Abergele churchyard.

An Up express is about to enter Penmaenrhos tunnel as it leaves Old Colwyn.

The castellated entrance to Penmaenrhos tunnel. Immediately after leaving the tunnel, heading towards Colwyn Bay, the railway passes under the 1983-built Tan-y-Lan viaduct which carries the new A55 Expressway into Colwyn Bay. The new road, which reflects the decline in railway travel, closely follows the railway to the Clwyd/Gwynedd border.

A goods train approaches Old Colwyn station as it heads towards Rhyl over a stone viaduct. Old Colwyn station opened in April 1884 as 'Colwyn'. Passenger services were withdrawn in 1952, but the station survived until 1964.

A view of the viaduct from the seaward side, the passenger train having just left Old Colwyn station on its way towards Colwyn Bay and Llandudno Junction.

LNWR 2–2–2–2 'Greater Britain' class Compound No. 2051 *George Findlay* enters Old Colwyn station with a stopping train to Chester in 1905.

An LNWR 'Precursor' 4–4–0 approaches Old Colwyn with a Chester train just before the outbreak of the First World War.

During the 1950s BR ran a summer service between Llandudno and Rhyl, using two coaches and an Ivatt 2–6–2 tank loco operated on the push-pull system. This train was called '*The Welsh Dragon*' and must have been the shortest named train operating. It is seen here at Colwyn Bay station, which opened in 1849 as 'Colwyn'. A new station, called 'Colwyn Bay', was opened in June 1907 with track widening and still exists today. A section of the Up platform has now been taken over by private enterprise and the old station buildings are used as a restaurant and model shop. A model railway is also on site.

The Up 'Irish Mail', headed by a pair of LNWR 2–4–0 locos, approaches mail pick-up apparatus near the pier a little west of Colwyn Bay station. The pier is still *in situ* but is in a rather dilapidated state.

An LMS poster advertising Colwyn Bay. The railway company was keen to exploit holiday traffic to the resort.

An LNWR 'Precursor'-hauled 'Irish Mail' train prepares to collect mailbags as it approaches Colwyn Bay on its way to Euston.

An LNWR 'George V' class 4–4–0 heads a Down express, possibly the 'Irish Mail', through Colwyn Bay on its way to Holyhead in 1914. The train is on the Down fast line and will probably not call at Llandudno Junction.

NWAY ROAD, COLWYN BAY.

An Up LNWR passenger train is seen on the slow line of the four-track section between Colwyn Bay and Llandudno Junction in the period before the First World War. The four tracks here were rationalized down to two in 1966. In 1983/4, the track west of Colwyn Bay was re-aligned, occupying land just to the right of the original formation, to make way for the £500 million A55 expressway, which runs parallel to the railway all the way through to Llandudno Junction and is a constant reminder of the primacy of road transport over rail in modern north Wales. The road, however, does provide a good vantage point to view steam-hauled 'North Wales Coast Express' trains, which run from Crewe to Holyhead, and provide a glimpse of the railway as it used to be.

A local train passes the site of Mochdre and Pabo station on 3 June 1966, the last year of steam operation on the north Wales coast. Mochdre and Pabo station was the last in Clwyd, heading west from Colwyn Bay to Llandudno Junction, the latter station being only a mile away. A station was sited here in 1889 and had timber platforms to the slow lines only. It had a short life, closing in 1931. Mochdre and Pabo does, however, have its place in railway history, being the site of the first water troughs anywhere in the world. Water troughs were placed here in October 1860, allowing nonstop pick-up of water for locomotive tenders, because the Post Office insisted that the 'Irish Mail' train should cover the 263½ miles between London and Holyhead at a high average speed. The Mochdre troughs were invented by John Ramsbottom, then Locomotive Superintendent of the LNWR, and water was taken from Mochdre stream, under an agreement with Lord Mostyn of Llandudno. So successful were these troughs that they were laid on the Up line as well as those on the Down. The Mochdre troughs worked well until problems of water supply from nearby railway reservoirs forced their movement to Aber (between Llanfairfechan and Bangor) in 1871.

SECTION TWO
LNWR Branches

Once the main Chester and Holyhead line had been established, the LNWR opened branches from the main line to serve towns and villages in the coastal hinterland. Some of these lines were rather important, serving market towns like Mold and Denbigh, while others served small villages like Dyserth. The longest branch was the line from Rhyl to Corwen (where it met the GWR line from Ruabon to Barmouth) and was nearly 29 miles long, while the shortest was only 1¼ miles in length, and was built to link the main-line Holywell station with the town of Holywell.

Over the years, a wide variety of motive power could be seen operating trains over these branches, from humble LNWR 2–4–2 tank engines to large 4–6–0 tender locomotives. The Prestatyn-Dyserth branch, however, operated its passenger services using steam railcars, which saved the expense of separate loco haulage on such a sparsely used line.

Sadly, like much of the railway system, all of these branches have closed, most ceasing to exist in the post-Beeching years of the 1960s, although a few had lost passenger services some years before.

An important branch ran from Foryd Junction, on the main Chester and Holyhead line just west of Rhyl, to Denbigh and Corwen. The first section of the line between Foryd Junction and Denbigh was opened as the Vale of Clwyd Railway on 5 October 1858, and absorbed into the London and North Western Railway in 1867. Foryd station, on the main CHR line, closed as early as April 1885, all trains starting and terminating at Rhyl. The section between Denbigh and Corwen, where the line met the GWR route from Ruabon to Dolgellau and Barmouth, was opened on 1 March 1862. The first station from Foryd Junction was at Rhuddlan, pictured here at the turn of the century. It appears to have been a substantial building and had a small staff. There was also another line which ran from Foryd, this connecting the CHR main line with an army camp some four miles inland at Kinmel Park. It was built during the First World War and used for military traffic until 1925, when it became an outlet line for the nearby St George's quarry, remaining open until February 1965. The line from Denbigh continued from Foryd to a pier at the mouth of the River Clwyd.

RHYL, ST. ASAPH, AND DENBIGH. Week days only.

	a.m.	a.m.		a.m.	a.m.		a.m.	p.m.		p.m.		p.m.		p.m.		p.m.		p.m.		p.m.	
Rhyl ....depart	7 40	8 30		9 10	10 55		12 2	1 7		4 20		5 33		6 35		7 15		8 50		10 15	
Rhuddlan		8 40	One class only.	9 19	11 4			3 14		4 27		5 40		6 37		7 19	First class only.	8 57		10 21	
St. Asaph	7 51	8 44		9 24	11 10		1 30	3 21		4 34		5 47		6 44		7 20		9 4		10 32	
Trefnant	7 58	8 50		9 30	11 16		1 42	3 27		4 40		5 54		6 50		7 35		9 10		10 40	
Denbigh ....arrive	8 9	8 55		9 35	11 25		1 50	3 35		4 48		6 2		6 53		7 43		9 19		10 51	

	a.m.		a.m.	a.m.	a.m.		p.m.		p.m.		p.m.		p.m.	p.m.		p.m.	p.m.		p.m.	
Denbigh ....depart	6 25		7 53	9 47	11 40		2 17		3 25		3 58		5 3	6 4		7 17	7 57		8 51	
Trefnant	6 31		8 1	9 55	11 46		2 23		3 30		4 5		5 9	6 11		7 23	8 3		8 57	
St. Asaph	6 37		8 7	10 0	11 50		2 29		3 35		4 9		5 15	6 17		7 30	8 10		9 3	
Rhuddlan	6 41		8 14	10 6	11 56		2 36		3 40		4 9		5 23	6 24		7 35	8 16		9 10	
Rhyl ....arrive	6 53		8 23	10 15	12 10		2 45		3 52		4 19		5 34	6 31		7 46	8 27		9 21	

An early twentieth-century LNWR timetable for the branch to Denbigh from Rhyl.

The first station on the line was at Rhuddlan. Its substantial main building is on the large platform. Access to the goods yard is visible beyond the platform, with two open wagons awaiting collection.

The main brick-built station building at Rhuddlan with a road overbridge crossing the railway, looking towards Rhyl.

Ex-LMS Hughes-Fowler 'Crab' 2–6–0 No. 42942 is in charge of a railtour along the Denbigh branch, organized by the Locomotive Club of Great Britain, on 24 September 1966.

The second station on the line from Rhyl to Denbigh was at St Asaph, with a very attractive main building.

The rather substantial brick-built waiting shelter on the Denbigh platform at St Asaph.

The large junction station at Denbigh, where the line from Mold met the Vale of Clwyd route. Denbigh could at one time provide a direct service to Chester, which meant that there was no need to travel to Rhyl for a connection to Chester, Crewe, London or the north-west of England on the CHR.

The importance of Denbigh station was reflected in the almost cathedral-like quality of its station building, as can be seen in this view. The line from Rhyl to Denbigh was closed to passengers on 19 September 1955, but remained open for freight until the end of 1967. Sadly, nothing of the line or Denbigh station now remains to show how important they once were.

The station building and platform canopy at Denbigh. Its large size only emphasized the importance of the place.

Denbigh was considered important enough to be provided with a small locoshed. It was a sub-shed of Rhyl (BR code 6K) and was provided with motive power from the parent shed's allocation. The little shed is seen here on 6 July 1935, with an ex-LNWR 2–4–2 tank loco and LMS 4F 0–6–0 tender engine. The shed was closed in 1957 but survives as a factory unit.

An ex-LNWR 2–4–2 tank, now LMS No. 6611, is pictured at the front of Denbigh shed on 6 July 1935.

Another ex-LNWR 2–4–2 tank loco, LMS No. 6669, being prepared for duty at Denbigh shed's coaling stage on 6 July 1935. These locos would have operated local trains between Rhyl and Denbigh.

Ex-LNWR 'Coal' engine 0–6–0, as LMS No. 8588, rests at the side of Denbigh shed on 6 July 1935. The engine would have worked freight traffic during this period.

LMS 4F 0–6–0 No. 4514 passing through Denbigh with a local freight train on 6 July 1935.

Denbigh was the junction of the line to Mold Junction and Chester. About seven miles east of Denbigh was the large station at Caerwys, seen here at the turn of the century. The line opened as the Mold and Denbigh Junction Railway on 12 September 1869 and was double track throughout. It closed on 30 April 1962. The station at Caerwys, however, still exists, serving as the offices of a timber mill.

An attractive view of the exterior of the important station at Mold, which served the thriving market town. The station yard appears to be busy, with an LNWR bus for railway passengers, and horse-drawn carts.

MOLD, COED TALON, AND BRYMBO.		Week days only. One class only.

Mold station not only served trains between Chester and Denbigh, but also services to the outskirts of Wrexham, as this old LNWR timetable shows.

The first station on the section from Denbigh to Corwen was at Llanrhaiadr, yet another substantial structure, as were all the stations along the line. It is seen here at the turn of the century and shows the staff, with their wives and children. Note the level crossing at the Denbigh end of the station.

A long LNWR train is seen running along the Vale of Clwyd line between Rhewl and Ruthin. The line ran through some attractive hill country, which was something of a contrast with the more rugged mountain terrain of Snowdonia, lying further west in Gwynedd.

A BR Standard class 4 4–6–0 hauls a light two-coach train through the Vale of Clwyd early in 1962, just before closure of the line to passengers. In the last century, the Great Western Railway was keen to take control of this line, as it would have given the Paddington company access to the Chester and Holyhead main line at Rhyl, and a possible route from its own line at Corwen to the main Irish Sea packet port at Holyhead. The LNWR, however, jealously guarded its interests and there was no way that its bitterest of rivals was going to have the Corwen–Rhyl line. Had the GWR taken over the line and obtained access to Holyhead, there is the possibility that the west Wales port it built at Fishguard for Irish traffic may never have been established.

Part of an LMS excursion advert showing fares and special arrangements for large parties.

Ruthin station in LNWR days. The station served the important market town. The platform canopy covers the whole platform, but was later cut back.

Ruthin station, looking towards Corwen. The cut-back station canopy can be seen in this view.

The signal-box at Ruthin, situated on the Corwen platform. Just in view on the left is the goods shed, freight traffic being fairly substantial, as befitted a market town.

A general view of Ruthin station, showing the main building, signal-box and goods shed. After closure of the line, the area was redeveloped and nothing of the railway now exists, except a yard crane mounted on a plinth, serving as a reminder of Ruthin's railway past.

BR Standard class 4 4–6–0 No. 75010 of Llandudno Junction locoshed (6G) departs from Ruthin station with a two-coach local service to Rhyl on a wet day in 1962.

Ewarth station, looking towards Corwen, after passenger services had been withdrawn. However, the line did see passenger trains after closure to regular services, 'North Wales Land Cruise' trains and other excursions using the line to gain access to the GWR route at Corwen for Barmouth on the Cambrian coast.

Nantclwyd station and staff at the turn of the century.

A derelict-looking Derwen station around 1962.

Derwen station again, looking towards Corwen.

Glynderwen station looking somewhat overgrown. This was the last station on the line from Rhyl before reaching the terminus at Corwen.

Opened in 1912, the Holywell Junction to Holywell Town branch was only a little over a mile long and was on a gradient of 1 in 27, making it one of the steepest lines worked by locomotives in Great Britain. There was an intermediate station called St Winefride's, situated some distance from the famous well. Trains started their journeys from a bay next to the side wall of the main building at Holywell Junction, at the Chester end of the station, the loco always placed at the main-line end of the formation. It was a magnet for railway enthusiasts who could enjoy a loco working hard as it climbed the branch. The picture shows the Holywell Town terminus on the opening day, judging by the number of people present and the bunting on the station approach road. The loco hauling the train is LNWR 2–4–2 tank No. 2519, which operated trains in the early days. These locos were replaced by LNWR 0–6–2 'Coal Tanks', and by LMS Ivatt 2–6–2 tanks in BR days. All were push-pull fitted to prevent the need for running round at termini.

HOLYWELL JUNCTION AND HOLYWELL TOWN.

Week days only.
One class only.

	a.m.		a.m. a.m. a.m.	a.m.		a.m.	p.m. p.m. p.m.		p.m. p.m. p.m.		p.m. p.m. p.m.		p.m. p.m. p.m.		a.m. a.m. a.m.	
Holywell Junction depart	7 25		8 15 9 10 10 5	11 55		12 50 1 25 2 25		3 55 5 30 6 5		6 45 7 20 8 35		9 15 10 30	
St Winefride			8 40			12 55		4		6 50			9 20	
Holywell Town arrive	7 35		8 43 9 15 10 13	12 3		12 58 1 33 2 33		4 3 5 38 6 13		6 53 7 28 8 43		9 23 10 38	
	a.m.		a.m. a.m. a.m.	p.m.		p.m. p.m. p.m.		p.m. p.m. p.m.		p.m. p.m. p.m.		p.m. p.m.	
Holywell Town depart	7 35		8 48 9 35 10 30	12 6		1 2 1 45		3 5 4 25 5 40 6 15		7 5 8 15 8 45		10 0 10 45	
St Winefride			8 51			1 6 1 51		4 29 6 19			10 5 10 48	
Holywell Junction arrive	7 45		8 58 9 45 10 40	12 16		1 12 1 53		3 15 4 35 5 50 6 26		7 15 8 25 8 55		10 10 10 55	

Timetable for the Holywell Junction and Holywell Town branch line.

46614. HOLYWELL: GENERAL VIEW.

Holywell was situated in a narrow valley packed with diverse industries: lead mining and copper smelting were important economic contributors, as were paper and flannel making. A 3 ft gauge tramway had been operating between Holywell and the River Dee at Greenfield to carry mined lead and limestone from the hills above the town. It was soon apparent that something better was required and, in 1864 the Holywell Railway Company proposed to build a line to connect with the CHR, a working agreement being reached with the LNWR. The scheme was, however, abandoned after four years. In 1906 the LNWR obtained authority to build the Holywell branch, but appeared to forget about it for a while. Once opened, the branch did much for the local economy. A general view of the town and its railway station can be seen here, with a two-coach train hauled by an LNWR tank leaving for Holywell Junction. In the distance the Wirral can be seen.

On opening day passengers are seen awaiting the arrival of a train from Holywell Junction. Goods facilities were also provided at the station, and the freight line to the sidings can be seen on the right of the picture.

Holywell Town station platform and waiting room in a photograph taken from the goods siding.

Holywell Town station and goods yard. The line down to Holywell Junction can be seen disappearing through the left-hand arch of the road overbridge, while the goods yard is situated beyond the right-hand arch.

Passengers leave the newly arrived train at Holywell Junction in LNWR days. The driving trailer is at the front of the formation.

Holywell Town station looking from the direction of Holywell Junction, with an LNWR 0–6–2 'Coal Tank' in charge of the one-coach train. To the left are wagons in the goods yard. Despite high hopes for the success of the little branch, passenger services declined fairly quickly after opening, a situation not helped by the fact that the LNWR actually ran a bus service to Holywell from the main line. It was therefore no real surprise when the line closed to passengers in 1954, and only survived for freight use until 1957. The junction was removed a year later and little now remains of Holywell Town station, except for a section of platform edge beneath the overbridge.

Constructed to tap lead and haematite mines in the Prestatyn Valley, the LNWR opened a three-mile, single-track branch between Prestatyn and Dyserth in 1869. From 1905 a passenger service was operated from a bay at the western end of the CHR station at Prestatyn to Dyserth, using steam railmotor cars. By 1928 three intermediate halts had been added. The steam railmotors continued to operate the passenger services until replaced by loco-hauled stock just before closure to passengers in 1930. Freight used the line until 1964, which continued as a private siding until 1973.

PRESTATYN AND DYSERTH.   Week days only. One class only.

		a.m.	a.m.	a.m.	a.m.	p.m.	p.m.		p.m.	p.m.		p.m.	p.m.	p.m.
Rhyl	depart		7 30	9 25	10 55	12 30	2 0		2 55	4 35		SS20	6 5	9 10
Prestatyn	depart	6 57	7 45	9 40	11 10	12 45	2 20		3 30	4 50		6 0	6 55	9 36
Chapel Street		7 1	7 49	9 44	11 14	12 49	2 24		3 34	4 51		6 4	6 59	9 39
Rhuddlan Road		7 4		9 47	11 17	12 52			3 37	4 57		6 7	7 2	9 43
Meliden		7 8	7 57	9 52	11 22				3 42			6 12	7 7	9 47
Dyserth	arrive	7 14	8 2	9 57	11 27	1 2	2 37		3 47	5 7		6 17	7 12	9 52
		a.m.	a.m.	a.m.	a.m.	p.m.	p.m.		p.m.	p.m.		p.m.	p.m.	p.m.
Dyserth	depart	7 17	8 5	10 10	11 55	1 5	2 40		4 0	5 15		6 25	7 15	9 56
Meliden		7 21	8 10	10 14	12 0	1 10			4 5	5 20		6 30	7 20	10 1
Rhuddlan Road		7 24	8 13	10 18	12 3				4 9	5 23		6 33		10 4
Chapel Street		7 27	8 15	10 20	12 5	1 15			4 11	5 25		6 35		10 7
Prestatyn	arrive	7 31	8 19	10 24	12 9	1 19	2 54		4 14	5 29		6 39	7 29	10 10
Rhyl	arrive		8 28	10 32	12 29	1 30	3 27		4 24	5 44		6 54	7 44	10 28

S—Saturdays only.

An LNWR timetable for the Prestatyn–Dyserth branch.

An LNWR steam railmotor runs along the attractive wooded Dyserth branch shortly after the opening.

An official photograph of the opening of one of the steam railmotors operating the Dyserth branch at Prestatyn. The train is full of passengers dressed in typical Edwardian fashions, the ladies in long dresses and the men sporting straw hats, toppers or caps. The guard looks well turned-out in his LNWR uniform.

A multi-coach train heads up the Dyserth branch, a very unusual sight even in the early years of passenger operation on the line.

A steam railmotor at Rhuddlan Road station in the early years of passenger operation. Rhuddlan Road was the first station on the line from Prestatyn.

A railmotor passes through a wooded section of the Dyserth branch.

A tank loco-hauled train approaches a deserted Rhuddlan Road Halt in the final year of passenger services on the Dyserth branch.

The train crew pose beside their steam railmotor at Meliden Halt during the first year of passenger operation.

Crew and a passenger pose for an official photograph at Meliden on the first day of operation on the Dyserth branch.

Another official photograph, this time at the terminus of the branch, Dyserth. In the background is the water tank to refresh locos after arriving at the terminus.

The terminus at Dyserth, complete with wooden station buildings. This view was taken just before closure to passengers, as the train is loco-hauled.

The goods yard at Dyserth, long after passenger services ceased. LMS 4F 0–6–0s of Rhyl shed generally handled goods traffic up the branch until closure. The track was lifted in 1980, but enthusiasts formed the North Clwyd Railway Association to try and re-open the line. Their efforts were partly rewarded when Rhuddlan Borough Council bought the trackbed and now it remains to be seen whether trains will, once again, run to Dyserth.

Rails to Wrexham

Wrexham was a very important point on the railway network in Clwyd, not least because the lines that met in the town served quarries, collieries, brickworks and steelworks which crowded the eastern part of the county (the old county of Flintshire). Such was the importance of east Flintshire that three of the post-Grouping companies the GWR, LMS and LNER, had railway routes into Wrexham. Incidentally, Wrexham was the furthest point west reached by the LNER and the King's Cross company only gained access to north Wales by virtue of the fact that the old Great Central Railway, which had become a constituent of the LNER in 1923, had taken control of the Wrexham, Mold and Connah's Quay Railway in 1905. The LMS, despite its virtual monopoly of traffic on the north Wales coast, had only a very minor role in Wrexham. Both the GWR and LNER had substantial stations in the town.

As a major industrial centre, Wrexham had the most complex railway system in Clwyd, most lines handling the myriad freight trains emanating from industrial sites and local passenger trains, which were just as important, taking the local population to their places of employment or to shopping centres. These passenger trains were usually handled by tank engines, like GWR 0–6–0 pannier tanks or Great Central Railway 4–4–2 tanks. All manner of locos handled freight traffic, much of which went to Connah's Quay for onward shipment.

With such a wide variety of traffic in the area, Wrexham was blessed with two locosheds, one, at Rhos Ddu, dealing with LNER traffic (BR code 84K), the other, at Croes Newydd (BR code 84J), supplying motive power for the GWR. The LNER shed was originally built by the WM&CQR and taken over by the GCR when that company bought the Welsh line. The shed at Rhos Ddu was officially closed in 1960, but was retained as a store for withdrawn ex-GWR engines until 1963. The GWR shed at Croes Newydd was the more important of the two, and it provided locos for sub-sheds at Bala, Penmaenpool, and Trawsfynydd (all in Gwynedd). Its allocation included 0–6–0 pannier tanks for local passenger work and pick-up goods traffic, 0–6–2 tanks, 2–6–0 tender engines, and the odd 'Manor' class 4–6–0. By the mid-1960s, as ex-GWR engines were withdrawn, ex-LMS 'Black 5' or 'Jubilee' 4–6–0s were allocated to the shed. Much of the railway system around Wrexham closed in the late 1960s and early 1970s, steam traction having been withdrawn a couple of years earlier, and the sheds were closed. The Rhos Ddu shed site is now occupied by factory units, while Croes Newydd shed was demolished in 1974/5 and is now a gypsy camp site.

Constructed by the Wrexham, Mold and Connah's Quay Railway, Hawarden station was situated on the Great Central Railway line to the Wirral and Chester. Hawarden was best known as the home of the Liberal prime minister, William Ewart Gladstone, who lived in a mansion nearby. He was involved in railway legislation, introducing so-called parliamentary trains, which stipulated that third-class passengers had to be carried in enclosed accommodation instead of open goods wagons then favoured by the railway companies, on proper passenger trains instead of goods trains, at a rate of not more than a penny a mile. The railway companies did not like these new regulations, and ran parliamentary trains at most unsociable hours, until they realized that even third-class passengers could be a good source of revenue.

Table 79 — CHESTER, CONNAH'S QUAY & SHOTTON, and HAWARDEN

An LNER timetable for trains through Hawarden station in January 1947.

The docks at Connah's Quay, which had been constructed by the WM&CQR and taken over by the GCR. In the second half of the nineteenth century, a rail connection was made with the LNWR's Chester and Holyhead Railway at its own Connah's Quay station. A variety of ships can be seen at the wharf, from steamers to sailing ships. The quay was important for the movement of raw materials from the steelworks, coal mines and brickworks in the Wrexham area, much of this freight traffic brought to the quay by the network of railways in east Clwyd.

Shotton (High Level) station on the GCR, which was absorbed by the LNER following the Grouping of 1923. The line ran between the Wirral and Wrexham and crossed the Chester and Holyhead Railway at right angles on an overbridge. Entrance to the CHR Low Level station was through High Level. Here, an ex-LNER (GCR) class C13 4–4–2 tank engine heads a stopping train from Seacombe to Wrexham on 26 August 1953. The line is still in existence, DMU trains operating between the Wirral and Wrexham.

An Edwardian view of Connah's Quay and Shotton station, supplied with a wooden platform and wooden buildings. It was situated on the WM&CQR line from Hawarden to Buckley Junction. It became GCR property in 1905, and transferred to the LNER in 1923.

Miles	**Down**	**Week Days only**													
		a.m	a.m	a.m		p.m	p.m		p.m	p.m		p.m			
	Wrexham (Central) ¶ ....dep	7 40	9 45	11 3	..	1 20	3 30	..	5 3	6 30	..	9 0	..	..	..
2¾	Marchwiel ¶	7 46	9 51	11 9	..	1 26	3 36	..	3 9	6 36	..	9 6	..	..	..
5¾	Bangor-on-Dee ¶	7 58	10 0	1118	..	1 35	3 45	..	5 19	6 45	..	9 15	..	..	..
8¾	Overton-on-Dee ¶	8 16	10 9	1126	..	1 43	3 53	..	5 27	6 53	..	9 23	..	..	..
12¾	Ellesmere 142, 144 .....arr	8 28	1021	1138	...	1 55	4 4	..	5 38	7 5	..	9 34	..	..	..
23¼	144 WHITCHURCH ....arr	9 11	..	12 7	..	2 39	4 34	..	6 14	7 45	..	1017	..	..	..
20¼	142 OSWESTRY "	9 6	1042	..	..	2 55	4 57	..	..	7 41	..	1010			

Miles	**Up**	**Week Days only**											
		a.m	a.m	a.m		a.m		p.m		p.m	p.m	p.m	
	144 OSWESTRY ....dep	7 40	8 20	..	..	1120	..	1 40	..	3 47	5 25	6 55	..
	142 WHITCHURCH "	2 55	8 17	..	9 55	..	non	..	2 5	..	4 5	6 50	..
—	Ellesmere ¶ ....dep	8 5	8 50	..	1025	..	12 0	..	2 40	..	4 20	5 50	7 25	..
4¾	Overton-on-Dee ¶	8 17	9 0	..	1035	..	1210	..	2 50	..	4 30	6 0	7 35	
7¾	Bangor-on-Dee ¶	8 26	9 8	..	1043	..	1218	..	2 58	..	4 38	6 8	7 43	
10¾	Marchwiel ¶ .... {9 25}	8 36	9 18	..	1053	..	1228	..	3 8	..	4 48	6 18	7 53	
12¾	Wrexham (Cen.) D 112 arr	8 43	9 25	..	11 0	..	1235	..	3 15	..	4 55	6 25	8 1	..

D Station for Holt (5¼ miles)

"Halts" at Hightown, between Wrexham (C.) & Marchwiel, at Sesswick, and at Pickhill, between Marchwiel and Bangor-on-Dee, at Cloy, between Bangor-on-Dee and Overton-on-Dee, at Trench and at Elson, between Overton-on-Dee and Ellesmere.

A January 1947 timetable for GWR services between Wrexham Central and Ellesmere. This was the old Cambrian Railways' foothold in the Wrexham area.

Buckley Junction station was really a misnomer as the Buckley Railway, from which it took its name, never carried any passenger trains. It was, however, the terminus of the WM&CQR line from Buckley to Buckley Junction. The Buckley Railway was one of the most intensively used lines in Wales, a single track serving brickworks and quarries strung out over the whole route. The line opened for goods on 7 June 1862, and was leased for 999 years to the WM&CQR from 30 June 1873. The northern section of the line closed in 1959, while the southern section, from Northop Hall Colliery to Buckley, closed on 5 July 1965. The passenger line from Buckley to Buckley Junction was opened on New Year's Day 1866 for goods and on the following 1 May for passengers. The line closed to passengers in February 1895 and to goods on 3 May 1965.

The Great Central Railway station at Wrexham Exchange. In the background is the GWR station, Wrexham General. Exchange station is on the Bidston line and was originally a terminus when opened in 1866. It became a through station in 1887, when an extension to Central station was completed. The station remains open today, along with Central, now referred to as 'General', as both Wrexham stations are now one.

Wrexham General station in the days before an overall roof was placed over the tracks. The main building was of Shrewsbury and Chester Railway design, the company being absorbed into the GWR following disputes with the LNWR at Chester. The little railway company looked to the larger Paddington company for 'protection' and the GWR was only too glad to take over the S&C, as it gave Paddington access to lucrative Merseyside traffic in competition with its Euston rival, something the LNWR had sought to avoid.

Table 78

SEACOMBE, NEW BRIGHTON, BIRKENHEAD, and WREXHAM

Week Days | **Sundays**

	am	am	am	a.m	a.m	a.m	p.m	p.m	p.m	p.m	p.m	p.m	p.m	p.m	p.m	p.m	p.m	p.m		am	a.m	p.m	p.m
				S	E	S	S	S	E	S	E	S	S	E	L	E	S	S					
Seacombe & Egremont dep	..	715	8 59	9 39	..	1128	11 28	1247	..	1 28	..	230	..	4Y30	..	5 7	5 34	6 27	729	813	9 25	..	..
Liscard and Poulton	..	720	8 9	9 43	..	1132	11 32	1251	..	1 32	..	234	..	4Y35	..	511	5 39	6 32	734	817	9 39	..	..
New Brighton ..... dep	..	655	759	9 22	..	1122	11 22	1239	..	1 19	..	222	..	4 22	..	455	5 28	6Y18	720	8 0	9 22	..	..
Liverpool H....... dep	..	7 2	758	9 29	..	1129	11 20	1258	..	1 18	..	220	..	4 25	..	458	5 26	6Y23	725	8 5	9 25	..	..
Birkenhead A ...... "	..	7 7	8 3	9 34	..	1125	11 25	1243	..	1 23	..	225	..	4 25	..	5 3	6733	6Y23	725	8 5	9 29	..	..
Bidston	..	726	814	9 48	..	1137	11 37	1255	..	1 38	..	240	..	4Y41	..	515	5 45	6 36	740	821	9 44	..	..
Upton	..	731	818	9 52	..	1141	11 41	..	..	1 43	..	245	..	4Y52	..	525	5 55	6 41	749	831	9 48	..	..
Storeton, for Barnston	..	737	824	9 58	..	1147	11 47	..	1 0	1 49	..	255	..	4Y56	..	529	5 59	6 51	753	835	9 58	..	..
Heswall Hills	..	741	828	10 2	..	1151	11 51	..	1 10	1 53	..	259	..	5 3	..	536	6 56	6 58	759	841	10 5	..	..
Neston and Parkgate	..	748	835	10 9	..	1158	11 58	..	1 17	2 0	..	2 6	..	5 V8	..	540	6 9	7 2	8 3	845	10 9	..	..
Burton Point E	..	752	839	1013	..	12 2	12 2	..	1 21	2 5	..	2 11	..	5 V8	..	546	6 15	7 7	8 8	851	1015	..	..
Hawarden Bridge Halt	620	758	845	1019	1152	12 8	12 8	..	1 29	2 13	..	314	..	5 V16	..	546	6 17	7 10	811	853	1020	..	..
Connah's Quay C { arr	622	8 0	847	1021	1152	1210	12 18	..	1 29	2 13	..	314	..	5 9	5V16	546	6 17	7 10	811	853	1020	..	..
{ dep	624	7 9	8 3	1023	1153	1213	12 20	..	1 31	2 16	222	252	316	422	510	534	548	6 19	722	814	929	1022	1116
Hawarden	630	716	8 9	1029	1159	1220	12 27	..	1 37	33 2	228	258	323	428	516	540	554	6 26	728	822	937	1028	1122
Buckley Junction	636	722	815	1035	12 5	1227	12 32	..	81 43	38 2	29	3 3	329	434	522	546	6 0	6 32	734	829	943	1034	1128
Hope (Exchange)	..	725	818	1038	..	1236	12 35	..	1 46	..	2 32	..	332	437	..	549	6 3	6 35	..	..	..	..	..
Pen-y-ffordd D	640	727	820	1040	12 9	1232	12 37	1 21	1 48	..	2 34	238	334	439	527	551	6 5	6 37	740	833	947	1038	1132
Hope Village	644	731	824	1044	1213	1236	12 41	1 61	1 52	..	2 42	242	338	443	531	555	6 9	6 41	743	837	951	1042	1136
Caergwrle Castle and Wells	647	734	827	1047	1216	1239	12 44	1 19	1 55	..	2 45	..	341	446	534	..	6 12	6 44	746	841	954	1045	1139
Cefn-y-bedd	651	738	831	1051	1219	1242	12 58	2 4	2 48	..	344	449	537	6 15	6 47	..	749	844	957	1048	1142		
Gwersyllt	655	742	835	1055	1224	1247	12 52	1 2	72 3	..	2 49	253	349	454	542	..	6 6	620	6 52	754	849	102	1053	1147
Wrexham (Exchange)	659	746	839	1059	1228	1251	12 58	1 5	1 12	7	2 53	257	352	458	546	..	6 19	6 59	..	758	853	106	1057	..
" (Central)... arr	7 2	749	842	..	11 2	1231	1254	12 59	1 34	2 10	..	2 56	3 0	355	5	549	..	8 1	856	109	11 0	1152		

Week Days | **Sundays**

Miles		a.m	a.m	a.m	a.m	a.m	a.m	p.m	p.m	p.m	p.m	p.m	p.m	p.m	p.m	p.m	p.m	p.m	p.m		a.m	a.m	p.m	p.m
								S		E	S	S			S	E	S	E	S					
	Wrexham (Central)...dep	6 15	6 27	7 7	725	8	3 9	35	1130	1250		1 35	2 35		3 48	4 25		5 26	6 16	27	7 25	8 20	9 20	1020
1	" (Exchange)...dep	6 18	6 30	710	729	8	6 9	38	1133	1253		1 38	2 38		3 53	4 28		528	6 13	6 30	7 28	8 23	9 23	1043
2½	Gwersyllt	6 23	6 35	715	733	8	11 9	43	1138	1258		1 43	2 43		3 56	4 33		533	6 18	6 35	7 33	8 28	9 28	1048
4½	Cefn-y-bedd	6 27	6 40	719	737	8	15 9	47	1142	1	2	1 47	2 47		4 0	4 40		538	6 29	6 39	7 37	8 32	9 32	1052
4¾	Caergwrle Castle and Wells	6 30	6 43	722	740	8	18 9	50	1145	1		1 50	2 50		4 4	4 44		541	6 25	6 42	7 40	8 35	9 35	1056
7½	Hope Village	6 33	6 48	725	743	8	21 9	53	1148	1		1 53	2 53		4 4	4 43		544	6 28	6 45	7 43	8 38	9 38	1058
7½	Pen-y-ffordd D	6 38	6 51	730	748	8	24 9	58	1153	1		1 58	2 58		4 4	4 48		549	6 33	6 50	7 48	8 43	9 43	11 3
9	Hope (Exchange)	6 41	..	733	752	8	27	10 1	1156	1	16				4 4	4 51		553	6 36	6 53	7 51	..	9 18	10 5
11	Buckley Junction	6 45	6 57	737	756	8	33	10 5	12 0	1	23	2 4		313	4 18	4 55		557	6 40	6 57	7 55	8 50	9 18	10 11
11	Hawarden	6 51	7 4	744	8	2 8	39	1010	12 5	1	29	2	42		313	4 16	5 0		6 2	6 46	7 3	8 0	8 55	9 28	10 01
13	Connah's Quay C { arr	6 56	7 9	749	8	7 8	44	1015	1210	1	30	2	15	2	315	4 25	5		6 7	6 51	7 8	8 5	9 0	9 29	10 0
13	{ dep	..	7 11	752	810	..		1017	1214	1	34	..		3 17	..	4 31		5 28	610	..	716	8 7	9 10	9 31
13½	Hawarden Bridge Halt	..	7 65	813	..	..		1019	1214	1	34	..		..	..	4 53		5 31	612	..	720	8 9	9 12	9 34
17	Burton Point E	..	7 18	1	829	..		1023	1226	1	41	..		3 25	4 39		537	619	..	725	8 22	9 18	9 40
19	Neston and Parkgate	..	7 24	7 825	..	..		1032	1227	1	47	..		3 38	4 44		5 40	632	..	733	8 32	9 24	9 47
23	Storeton, for Barnston	..	7 31	813	836	..		1038	1233	1	53	..		3 44	4 55		5 50	632	..	739	8 38	9 36	10 0
26	Upton	..	7 40	822	841	..		1047	1242	2	0	..		3 47	..		6 1	641	..	748	8 45	9 40	10 2
27½	Bidston	..	7 47	826	846	..		1052	1246	2	9	..		3 52	..		6 6	6 45	..	752	8 49	9 45	10 5
30½	Birkenhead A ... arr	..	7 59	839	859	..	11 8	1259	2 28			5u19		6u19	7 6		8 89	..	10 8	1028	10 48	..	10 8	..
32	Liverpool H... arr	..	8 4	844	9 4	..	1113	1	4 2	13		5u24		6u24	713		813	9 13	..	1013	..	10 53	..	1013	..
31½	Hawarden "	..	8 14	844	9 4	..	1112	1	4 2	32		5u23		6K24	712		812	9 12	..	1013	..	10 52	..	1016	..
29	Liscard and Poulton	..	7 51	831	831	..	1056	1251	2	13		3 56		5 10		6 11	652	..	757	8 49	9 49	9 49	..
30½	Seacombe & Egremont arr	..	7 55	835	855	..	10 0	1255	2	17		4 0		5 14		6 15	656	..	8 1	8 53	9 53	9 53	..

A Hamilton Square.   B Station for Burton and Puddington   C Connah's Quay and Shotton   D Station for Leeswood   E or £ Except Saturda
H Central (Low Level).   J Arr. 3 minutes earlier.   K 8 mins. later on Sats.   L 5 mins. earlier on Sats.   K Arr. 9 mins. earlier on Sats.
B or S Sats. only.   J 9 mins. later on Sats.   V 2 mins. earlier on Sats.   Y 2 mins. later on Sats.   Z 8 mins. earlier on Sats.

An LNER timetable for trains from Seacombe to Wrexham, operating over ex-GCR metals through Shotton.

At Rhos station, on the short branch from Wrexham Central, ex-GWR 0–6–0 pannier tank No. 1635 heads a local freight train. These little tank engines were a common sight on local freight and passenger trains in the Wrexham area, all being shedded at Croes Newydd.

Brymbo Junction, where the line to Brymbo left the joint GC/GWR line to Buckley.

The GWR station at Brymbo, which served a steelworks in the town. Both of these have now sadly disappeared. The station was part of the Brymbo–Minera line which opened between Brymbo and Coed Poeth in July 1847 for goods traffic only, and to passengers on 15 November 1897. A line from Coed Poeth to Berwig was opened to passengers in June 1905. Withdrawal of passenger services between Wrexham General, Brymbo and Berwig took place on New Year's Day 1931. The line survived for freight traffic between Brymbo West Junction and Minera until full closure on 1 January 1972. The line was originally incorporated as the North Wales Mineral Railway on 6 August 1844, amalgamated with the Shrewsbury, Chester and Oswestry Railway on 30 June 1845, and formed part of the Shrewsbury and Chester Railway on 28 August 1846, becoming part of the GWR from 1 September 1854.

A local train calls at Brymbo General station on a private charter, with a GWR 0–6–0 pannier tank in charge.

A section of the GWR line at Brymbo.

A section of the line between Brymbo and Berwig.

A GWR 0–4–2 tank loco waits at Berwig station during the winter before the outbreak of the First World War. Berwig station has a pagoda-style waiting shelter, typical of those used by the GWR for its minor stations. Berwig was to see passenger trains for only twenty-six years, the line obviously being not very profitable for the GWR.

SECTION FOUR

GWR Lines

In addition to local trains serving Wrexham, the GWR had two other important routes within Clwyd. The most important was the main line between Paddington and Birkenhead. A section of this line, between Shrewsbury and Saltney Junction, from where the GWR had running powers over the Chester and Holyhead line to gain access to Chester General station, ran along the eastern edge of the county. Famous as the route of the Paddington–Birkenhead expresses, none of the famous 'Star' and 'King' class 4–6–0s operated these trains beyond Wolverhampton, the line not being deemed suitable for such heavy engines. 'Castle' class 4–6–0s did, however, appear on these trains through Clwyd in the mid-1950s. As steam declined in the early 1960s, ex-LMS 'Jubilee' or 'Black 5' 4–6–0s often headed these trains between Chester and Shrewsbury. This line still exists, but no longer carries express trains, these having been withdrawn in 1967, and only DMU or 'Sprinter' trains now operate local services between Chester and Wolverhampton.

The other important line was the Ruabon–Barmouth route, which linked the Wrexham area with the Cambrian Coast line. This line ran through some of the most attractive of Clwyd's countryside, and was popular with tourists, who could use the line to visit places like Llangollen and Corwen, or walk through the hills of the Vale of Llangollen. During the summer months, local services were augmented by expresses to Barmouth and numerous excursions to beauty spots along the route. Local trains were hauled by 0–6–0 pannier tanks or 2–6–2 Prairie tanks, while excursions and express trains would be in the hands of GWR 2–6–0s or 'Manor' class 4–6–0s. The Ruabon–Barmouth line closed in the mid-1960s, but a section in the Llangollen area has since been re-opened by the Llangollen Railway Preservation Society, bringing steam trains back to this attractive part of Clwyd.

A turn-of-the-century view of Chester Street, Saltney, with an open-top electric tram running down the centre of the road. Trams were another form of rail transport common across Britain up to the 1950s. In the background, on the bridge that crosses the street, is the GWR Chester–Shrewsbury main line Saltney station, the entrance being on the left of the picture.

Saltney was the first station reached after leaving the Chester–Holyhead line at Saltney Junction. The GWR had running powers over the CHR to gain access to Chester General station. In fact, the line from Shrewsbury reached Chester two years before the CHR opened in 1848. At Chester, however, the Shrewsbury and Chester Railway ran into trouble with the LNWR. Its managing director, Captain Mark Huish, who wished to maintain the Euston company's monopoly of north-west of England traffic, did everything he could to keep the S&B out of Chester, including having the ticket collector of the S&B physically ejected from the station. Alarmed by the behaviour of Captain Huish, the S&B, along with the Shrewsbury and Birmingham Railway, which was also having difficulty with the 'good' captain over access to Birmingham, sought a merger with the Great Western Railway, which had not even reached the industrial Midland town by then. The GWR, seeing a chance to challenge the LNWR in its own territory, agreed to the merger and the two Shrewsbury companies became part of the Paddington empire from 1 September 1854. The GWR was then able to operate express and freight services to Chester and Birkenhead from Paddington, much to the annoyance of the LNWR.

Rosset station on the GWR main line between Chester and Shrewsbury. Having taken control of the S&C, the GWR gained its own main line in Clwyd, albeit over only a very small part of the eastern end of the county. The county, therefore, benefited by having a choice of routes to London. However, the LNWR line to Euston was shorter than the Paddington route.

Balderton station on the main Birkenhead–Paddington line.

Wrexham General, the GWR main-line station.

Gresford station, with ex-GWR Hawksworth two-cylinder 'County' class 4–6–0 No. 1024 *County of Pembroke* at the head of the Chester–Shrewsbury section of the Birkenhead–Paddington express, which had left Birkenhead Woodside at 2.35 p.m. on 7 August 1957. The train would have left Woodside station behind an ex-LMS 2–6–4 tank, to be replaced at Chester by the 'County' class loco for the journey to Wolverhampton, where it in turn would be replaced by a 'King' class 4–6–0 for the run to Paddington. The 'Kings' were considered too heavy to run any further north than Wolverhampton at this time, although they did eventually reach Shrewsbury, and Wolverhampton's Stafford Road shed had an allocation of two-cylinder locos, such as 'Hall' or 'Grange' 4–6–0s, as well as the 'Counties', for this work. Gresford had a large colliery and is remembered as the scene of one of the worst mining accidents in Britain when, in 1934, 265 miners were killed in a pit explosion. A cage wheel marks the spot of the disaster and acts as a memorial to the men who died.

Johnstown and Hafod station in the course of reconstruction, or is it demolition?

Ruabon station, which was a junction of the main GWR line between Chester and Shrewsbury and the three-mile line to Legacy, known as the Ponkey branch, which was opened to serve Henry Dennis' Wrexham colliery. The branch was opened for goods traffic as far as Aberderfyn in August 1881, and from Aberderfyn to Legacy in August 1876. The line between Aberderfyn and Legacy was opened to passengers in June 1905, although there were no passenger trains to Aberderfyn from Ruabon. The line closed as early as 1917, although the section between Ruabon (Gardden Lodge Junction) and Aberderfyn remained open until 1964. Ruabon was also a junction with the GWR line to Dolgellau, where it made a head-on connection with the Cambrian Railways line from Barmouth Junction on the Cambrian Coast line.

One of the county's most attractive railway routes was the line between Ruabon and Barmouth Junction, the section between Ruabon and Corwen being in Clwyd. Acrefair station, with its signal-box in the left foreground, is set against the Clwyd hills. Between here and Llangollen, there were stations at Trevor and Sun Bank Halt. An accident occurred in the area between Trevor and Sun Bank when a goods train, hauled by GWR 2–6–0 No 6315, was wrecked after the Llangollen branch of the Shropshire Union Canal broke its banks and washed away the railway embankment, leaving a gap 40 ft deep and over 100 yd long.

ISSUED ON ANY DAY FROM
10th APRIL to 26th OCTOBER, 1963
Available for one Week from date of issue
provide UNLIMITED TRAVEL in
VALLEY OF THE DEE

| SECOND CLASS FARE | 27/6 | SECOND CLASS FARE |

Children under Three years of age, Free; Three and under Fourteen years of age, Half-fare.

CHESTER
WREXHAM
CORWEN RUABON
BALA LLANGOLLEN
DOLGELLAU

AREA No. 14

(See overleaf for details of THE CAMBRIAN COAST AREA)

SEVEN-DAY HOLIDAY RUNABOUT TICKET FOR BICYCLES, DOGS, ETC.

Tickets for Bicycles, Dogs, etc., accompanying passengers are issued at the undermentioned charges

Bicycles	...	...	...	...		
Dogs	...	...	...	Not	13s. 9d.
Perambulators			folded	
Invalid Chairs under 60lbs. in weight		
Tandems, Mopeds and Motor Scooters (less than 100 c.c.)			20s. 8d.

Tickets are also issued for Mopeds and Motor Scooters (over 100 c.c.) at the full Second Class passenger charge.

Tickets can be obtained at the principal Stations and Agencies within the area covered by the Ticket.
Tickets available for break of journey at all intermediate Stations.
No allowance or extension of date can be granted on these tickets in consequence of there being no Sunday service in certain areas.
Holiday Runabout Tickets are not available on Road Motors.
Upon expiry the Holiday Runabout Ticket must be delivered to the Railways' Officials.
Luggage allowances are as set out in the Commission's Publications and Notices applicable to British Railways.
For further information apply to any of the Stations, and Agencies or to Mr. O. VELTOM, District Superintendent, Shrewsbury (Telephone Shrewsbury 3614, Extension 2238).

March, 1963.

BRITISH RAILWAYS

Sc. 25/03.   Printed in Great Britain by G. R. Griffith Ltd., Chester

The attractive nature of the line had long been recognized by the railway companies, and even BR advertised the line widely, including offers for cheap runabout tickets, as in this example from 1963.

Perhaps the most attractive station on the line was at the important resort town of Llangollen. It lay high above the River Dee, which ran parallel at this point. An unusual feature was the passenger foot-bridge. The staircase from the main platform was inside the main building, while the staircase on the opposite platform was cantilevered over the river.

Llangollen was provided with long platforms to cater for excursion trains, which were a regular summer feature. The Corwen end of the station was provided with waiting rooms for the use of excursion passengers.

Rushing through Llangollen with a train for Barmouth is a GWR Churchward 2–6–0. Through expresses to the Cambrian coast were a common sight at Llangollen during the summer, 'Manor' class 4–6–0s sharing the duties with Churchward Moguls.

WESTERN REGION

Llangollen International Musical Eisteddfod

Tuesday, 11th July to Sunday, 16th July
1961 (INCLUSIVE)

Half-Day Excursion Bookings

FROM UNDERMENTIONED STATIONS

Forward by any train leaving after 9-30 a.m.   Return by any train on day of issue.

STATIONS	Return Fares Second Class		STATIONS	Return Fares Second Class
	s. d.			s. d.
†ARTHOG	8/9		†DOLGELLAU	7/6
BALA			†DRWSYNANT	6/3
†BARMOUTH	4/3		†GLAN LLYN HALT	4/9
†MORFA MAWDDACH	9/3		GLYNDYFRDWY	1/9
BERWYN HALT	9/-		†GWERSYLLT	2/6
†BONTNEWYDD	8*		LLANDDERFEL	3/6
BONWM HALT	6/9		LLANDRILLO	3/-
CARROG	2/3		†LLANGOWER HALT	4/6
CORWEN	2/-		†LLANUWCHLLYN	5/-
CYNWYD	2/3		†PENMAENPOOL	8/-
	2/6			

†—No Suitable Train Service on Sundays.   *—Cheap Day Fares.

Children under Three years of age, Free; Three and under Fourteen years of age, Half-fare.
(Fractions of 1d. charged 1d.)

TICKETS CAN BE OBTAINED IN ADVANCE AT BOOKING STATIONS.

HOLIDAY RUNABOUT TICKETS AVAILABLE FOR SEVEN DAYS
ARE ISSUED GIVING UNLIMITED TRAVEL IN SPECIFIED HOLIDAY AREAS.

FOR DETAILS OF TRAIN SERVICES BETWEEN BARMOUTH AND
LLANGOLLEN—SEE OTHER SIDE.

For further information apply to any of the Stations and Agencies, or to Mr. O. VELTOM, District
Traffic Superintendent, Shrewsbury (Telephone Shrewsbury 3614, Extn. 42); Mr. W. R. STEVENS, Divisional
Traffic Manager, Cardiff.

Paddington Station, W.2.
June, 1961.

J. R. HAMMOND,
General Manager.

Se 25/1349   Printed in Great Britain by G. R. Griffith Ltd., Chester.

In 1946 the Llangollen International Musical Eisteddfod was established and the railways advertised special excursions for the event, providing a good source of revenue for both the GWR and BR.

A general view of Llangollen, with the station and railway in the bottom left of the picture. As well as the station, Llangollen had a large goods yard beyond the station in the direction of Corwen, the goods shed being visible at the bottom left of the picture. This goods yard handled freight from all parts of the UK, including coal and coke, manufactured goods, minerals and fertilizers, agricultural produce and livestock, the Vale of Llangollen being an important farming area. As well as receiving goods, Llangollen also despatched slate from the nearby Oernant Quarry, timber from local forests, farm livestock and general goods, under railway 'common-carrier' obligations. The yard itself was served by between one and four trains a day, including pick-up goods trains, operating, for example, between Ruabon and Bala, and fast goods trains operating to and from the Cambrian coast line, these only calling at important yards like Llangollen. As well as the goods yard, goods facilities were provided at a short siding at the Ruabon end of the main platform, behind the signal-box. The little siding was known as the 'Horse Landing' and was used for goods which were conveyed by passenger train.

The next station from Llangollen, in the direction of Corwen, was Berwyn, sandwiched between the A5 Holyhead road, which ran behind the station, and the Dee, which is below the station, opposite the single line. The large mock-Tudor main building gives the station an air of importance that it did not warrant, as only local services called there.

A BR advert offering excursions along the Ruabon–Barmouth line for Whit Monday 1964.

Glyndyfrdwy station, with a local train hauled, no doubt, by the ubiquitous GWR 0–6–0 pannier tank, departing for Corwen. The sidings serving the station handled significant quantities of slate traffic from local quarries, these being linked to the station by a narrow-gauge tramway.

A GWR train crosses a lattice-girder viaduct as it approaches Corwen in the early years of this century. The line between Ruabon and Corwen was built in two separate stages, the first being the Vale of Llangollen Railway, which had been incorporated on 1 August 1859. This line, from Ruabon to Llangollen, was opened on 1 December 1861 to goods traffic and 2 June 1862 to passengers. The second stage, between Llangollen and Corwen, was incorporated as the Llangollen and Corwen Railway on 6 August 1860 and opened to both passenger and goods traffic on 1 May 1865. The remainder of the line, from Corwen to the head-on connection with Cambrian Railways at Dolgellau, was opened in stages between April and August 1868. The whole line came under GWR control from 1 July 1896. When Cambrian Railways was absorbed by the GWR in 1922, trains operating over the line between Ruabon and Dolgellau continued through to Barmouth, on the Cambrian coast line. The LNWR line from Rhyl and Denbigh actually reached Corwen first, in October 1864. The section of the Corwen to Bala line between the original Corwen station of the LNWR and the new C&B station was opened in May 1865 and used by LNWR trains as well as those from Llangollen. The line between Llangollen Goods Junction and Bala Junction was closed on 13 December 1964, a few months before schedule, because flooding near Dolgellau prevented running of all trains. The whole line from Ruabon closed on 1 April 1968, but this was not to be the end for a section of the railway.

The handsome exterior of the jointly owned (LNWR and GWR) Corwen station. The station was opened in May 1865, the GWR always being the senior partner, although station staff were employed jointly. Among the facilities at Corwen was a two-road locoshed and turntable. In the early years of the line from Ruabon to Corwen, the shed supplied all required locos, but its importance declined when Croes Newydd shed at Wrexham was opened in 1902, and the GWR stopped using it in 1927. In 1921 the shed's allocation was only six locos: four 0–6–0 saddle tanks, a 2–4–0 and a 'Dean Goods' 0–6–0. Corwen ceased to be a junction for passengers as early as 1953, when services were withdrawn between Ruthin and Corwen, although excursion trains continued to use the line until September 1961.

Down — Week Days only

	ngt a.m a.m	a.m a.m a.m	p.m	a.m a.m a.m p.m	a.m p.m	p.m p.m p.m
13 London (Pad.) ... dep	12 5	.. .. 6 0	..	.. 9R10 11R10	11R10	2 10 4 10
108 Birmingham A. "	4 10	.. 7 40	..	8 36 11R56 1R43	1843	4 45 6 52
112 Shrewsbury (Gen.) "	3 46	.. 5 50	..	10 45 11 10 2R58	2R58	4 18 6 3 55
112 Manchester (Ex.) "	.. ..	6 30 7 50	..	10 25 11 45 ..	1 35	4 30 5 55
112 Birkenhead (W.) "	.. .. 6 30	7 10 8 40	..	11 40 12 25 1 10	2 35	3713 5 7 12
112 Chester (General) "	.. 7 10	8 40	..	12 22 1 15 1 50	3 17	4 20 5 50 7 55
Ruabon ... dep	7 0 .. .. 7 15 8 25	9 31	..	1 20 2 10 3 45	4 0	5 7 7 0 9 34
Acrefair	7 5 .. .. 7 21 8 30	9 36	..	1 26 2 16	4 5	5 12 6 9 39
Trevor	7 .. .. 7 25 8 33	9 39	..	1 29 2 19	4 8	5 15 10 9 42
Sun Bank Halt	.. .. 8 38		..			
Llangollen	7 15 .. .. 7 35 8 42	9 48	..	1 38 2 30 3 58	4 16	5 22 7 20 9 50
Berwyn	.. .. 7 40	9 53	..	1 46 2 35	4 25	7 26 Dd
Glyndyfrdwy	.. .. 7 49	10 2	..	1 55 2 42	4 35	7 35 10 3
Carrog	.. .. 7 55	10 7	..	2 0 2 47	4 41	7 40 10 9
Corwen 514	.. .. 8 5	10 15	..	2 10 2 55 4 20	4 53	7 50 1015
Cynwyd	.. .. 8 10	10 20	..	2 15 3 0	5 0	7 55 1020
Llandrillo	.. .. 8 17	10 25	..	2 20 3 6	5 5	8 0 1025
Llandderfel	.. .. 8 23	10 32	..	2 26 3 12	5 11	8 6 1031
Bala 141 arr	.. .. 8 45	10 55	..	2 36 3 39 4 50	5 21	8 27 1041
dep	.. .. 8 30	10 30	..	3 15 4 30		8 5
Llanuwchllyn	.. .. 8 51	10 56	..	3 38 Dd		8 29
Drws-y-Nant	.. 8 0 9 8	11 15	..	3 55 Dd 5 15		8 46
Bontnewydd	.. 9 18	11 25	..	4 5 Dd 5 24		8 56
Dolgelley	.. 8 19 9 30 9 31	11 39	1 45	4 17 5 21 5 32	6 18	9 6
Penmaenpool	.. 9 45	11 44	1 50	4 22 Dd	6 23	9 12
Arthog	.. 8 48 9 58	11 57	2 3	4 35	6 36	9 25
Barmouth Junc. 146	.. 8 51 10 2	12 0	2 6	4 38 5 39	6 39	9 30
Barmouth arr	.. 8 57 10 8	12 8	2 12	4 45 5 45	6 45	9 35
146 Pwllheli arr	.. 1055	2 0	4 10	6 27 7 11	8 12	..

Up — Week Days only

	a.m a.m	a.m a.m	a.m a.m	a.m	a.m a.m	p.m p.m p.m	p.m p.m p.m p.m p.m
146 Pwllheli dep	.. ..	.. ..	5 50 7 45	..	1025 1130	.. 1245	3 45 .. 6 40 6 40
Barmouth dep	.. ..	.. ..	7 18 9 20	10 10	1250 1 12	2 35	5 46 7 15 8 50 9 40
Barmouth Junction	.. ..	.. ..	7 24 9 31	10 16	1256 1 18	2 41	5 52 7 25 8 55 9 45
Arthog	.. ..	.. ..	7 27 9 34	10 19	1 0	2 44	5 55 7 28 8 58 9 48
Penmaenpool	.. ..	.. ..	7 39 9 46	10 32	1 14 1230	2 57	6 8 7 41 9 11 10 1
Dolgelley	.. ..	7 30	7 45 9 51	10 40	1 18 1 38	3 4 4 25	6 12 7 47 9 16 10 6
Bontnewydd	.. ..	7 40	7 52	10 45	1 44	3 11 4 36	7 57
Drws-y-Nant	.. ..	7 52	8 5	10 58	1 55	3 24 4 51	8 10
Llanuwchllyn	.. ..		8 20	11 18	2 8	3 38	8 25
Bala D arr	.. ..	7 17	8 30	11 25	2 8	3 25 3 45	5 50 8 33
dep	.. ..		8 42	11 40	2 26	3 33 4 0	5 58 8 52
Llandderfel	.. ..	7 25	8 47	11 45	2230	3 39 4 6	6 4 8 58
Llandrillo	.. ..	7 31	8 52	11 50		3 45 Kk	6 9 9 2
Cynwyd	.. ..	7 37	9 0	11 58	2 40	3 54 4 20	6 20 9 8
Corwen 514	.. ..	7 45	9 5	12 3		4 24 29	6 27 9 14
Carrog	.. ..	7 56	9 10	12 8		4 6 4 35	6 31 9 20
Glyndyfrdwy	.. ..	8 2	9 16	12 22	3 2	4 15 Kk	p.m 6 40
Berwyn	7 35	8 10 9 10	9 26			4 23 4 55	5 40 6 46 9 36
Llangollen	7 35	8 17 9 10	9 26		3 2	4 23 4 55	5 40 6 46 9 36
Sun Bank Halt							
Trevor	7 44	8 25 9 19	9 35 Hh	12 30		4 32 5 5	5 47 6 54 9 45
Acrefair	7 48	8 30 9 23		12 35		4 36 5 10	5 51 6 58 9 50
Ruabon 138, 112 arr	7 53	8 36 9 28	9 43	12 40	3 20	4 42 5 15	5 57 7 4 9 57
Chester (Gen.) arr	8 52	9 19	10 41	1 21	4 11	5 226	7 14 9 15 10 14
108 Birkenhead (W.) "	9 40	9 57	11 36	2 10	4 50	6 117 1	7 54 9 57 12 3
112 Manchester (Ex.) "	10 0	11 15	1826		6643	8 57	8 57 1054 3X50
112 Shrewsbury (G.) "	9 12	10 34	1R37	4 26		6 12	8 15 1X35
119 Birmingham (S. L.) "	10 47		11R54	3 R 0	6R53	7 48	1049
112 London (Pad.) "	2 15		2R35	5R40	8R40	1145	5*40

Footnotes

A Snow Hill	Hh Stops to set down on informing Guard at Llangollen	X Morning time. Via Wrexham.
B Arr 1 22 p.m on Sats.	K Except Sunday morns.	Z Dep. 3 30 p.m on Saturdays
b Arr 6 50 p.m on Saturdays	Kk Stops to set down from Bala, Llanuwchllyn, and beyond on informing Guard at Bala Junction	z Calls when required to take up for beyond Ruabon on notice being given at the Station
D Passengers to and from Bala change at Bala 5 unc. by most of the Trains	L Dep 12 30 p.m on Saturdays	* Morning time
Dc Calls to set down from beyond Ruabon on informing Guard at Ruabon	R Restaurant Car Train	† Arr. 5 minutes earlier
E or E Except Saturdays	S or S Saturdays only	‡ Arr. 3 27 p.m on Saturdays
		B Third class only

¶ "Halts" at Bonwm, between Carrog and Corwen, at Llangower and Flag Station, between Llandderfel and Llanuwchllyn, at Llys and at Garneddwen between Llanuwchllyn and Drws-y-Nant, at Wnion between Drws-y-Nant and Bontnewydd, and at Dolserau between Bontnewydd and Dolgelley.

OTHER TRAINS between Barmouth Junc. and Barmouth see page 146

A GWR timetable for services between Ruabon and Barmouth in January 1947. During the summer the number of trains over the route increased substantially, with services to Barmouth and extra trains to Llangollen.

Perhaps it seems inappropriate that a work on railways in old photographs should include pictures from the preservation era, but those featuring the Llangollen Railway are now, in themselves, historical. Here, ex-LMS 'Jinty' 0–6–0 tank loco No. 7298 waits at the locoshed at Llangollen to take out the tenth anniversary service in 1985.

At Llangollen station, the 'Jinty' tank backs under the roadbridge before running round its train for the inaugural run of the tenth anniversary train.

In 1985, the Llangollen Railway had only a little over a mile of track on which to operate its services, and the 'Jinty' tank runs around its train in preparation for the return to Llangollen after covering that stretch. Nowadays the Llangollen Railway has six miles of route available. The Llangollen preservation project started in 1975, when the Flint and Deeside Railway Society occupied the derelict and overgrown Llangollen station. The initial aim was to open a preserved railway between Llangollen and Corwen, an aim the railway society hopes to achieve, and it is coming closer to achieving that goal all the time. From 1975, track had been laid within the station complex, repair work on the station had been carried out, and a small engine shed with repair shop had been established. By 1981, a mile-long section of track had been opened. By the end of 1985, the line reached the next station from Llangollen at Berwyn, a distance of some two miles. The line opened to passengers in 1981, and has seen a steady increase in passengers over the years. Its value to the tourist economy of the area was recognized by the EC and the Wales Tourist Board, which have provided funds for the railway to complete the line to Corwen. The Llangollen Railway is one of the most friendly preserved railways. Everyone seems willing to chat and the welcome is very warm. All of those who work on the line are enthusiastic about it and I would certainly recommend a visit.

One of the Llangollen Railway's major acquisitions was ex-Western Region 'Manor' class 4–6–0 No. 7822 *Foxcote Manor*, obtained from the old station at Oswestry in October 1985, where it had been since its purchase from a Barry scrapyard by local enthusiasts. The loco had still to be restored, but the Llangollen Railway set about the task, and on 10 April 1988 she is seen ready to depart from Llangollen with her first public passenger train since withdrawal by BR in the 1960s. She is a credit to all those who strived to put her back in working order. The railway also had a second 'Manor', No. 7828 *Odney Manor*, but she is now on the East Lancashire Railway.

Foxcote Manor departs from the well-restored Llangollen station with the second train of its first day in service since restoration.

A rear view of *Foxcote Manor* as it heads from Llangollen to Berwyn on 10 April 1988.

Foxcote Manor at the attractively sited Berwyn station, with the River Dee below. The loco is on the viaduct and about to move empty stock into the loop beyond the station before returning to Llangollen. If the picture had been included in the section of old photos and dated sometime in the 1950s, it is doubtful that anybody would have been surprised, as the loco was regularly seen in the area at the head of Ruabon–Barmouth trains. Indeed, *Foxcote Manor* was given a very important role in August 1963 when, along with another preserved 'Manor', No. 7819 *Hinton Manor* (now on the Severn Valley Railway), she double-headed the Royal Train from Barmouth to Chester.

Railway Road Transport

The railway companies were aware of the value of local road networks as a means of connecting outlying villages with the railway, and both the LNWR and GWR operated bus services in Clwyd to carry passengers between their homes and local stations. The railway companies also operated fleets of lorries to carry goods between freight depots and customers, thereby offering a door-to-door service.

In the early years of the twentieth century, the railway companies were very active in this field, but competition by private bus and lorry operators after the First World War meant that many of these services were lost to private firms, and most had gone by the 1930s. Direct road competition to the railways, particularly in the shape of the long-distance motorcoach and heavy lorries, did much damage to the railways in Clwyd and elsewhere after the Second World War, causing closure of much of the system. Thus, it could be argued that the railways had sown the seeds of their own demise.

An LNWR double-decker bus service ran between Connah's Quay and Mold stations, providing a railway company service at Northop.

An official view of the LNWR bus operating the Connah's Quay to Mold service.

Before the opening of the Holywell Junction to Holywell Town branch line, the LNWR operated a single-deck bus service from the main CHR station at Holywell to the inland town. Even after the little branch had opened, the railway company still ran its bus service and, it could be argued, sabotaged its own train services. Here, the little bus is full as it makes ready to depart from Holywell Town.

A full LNWR double-decker on the Connah's Quay–Flint–Northop–Mold route, with another similar vehicle in the distance.

As well as providing bus services, the railway companies also operated lorries to provide a door-to-door service between goods yards and customers in an effort to generate freight business for themselves. Here, a loaded LNWR steam lorry, probably a Foden unit, is operating a goods service between Holywell, on the Chester and Holyhead main line, and Holywell Town.

Not only did the LNWR operate bus services in Clwyd – the GWR did the same. One such service operated from Corwen to the surrounding villages, and during the 1920s and 1930s a bus service ran from Corwen to Llangollen on Sundays to connect with trains to Ruabon, no Sunday rail service then operating between Llangollen and Dolgellau, except during the summer. One of the GWR buses is seen outside Corwen station in the early years of this century.

Miniature Railways and Tramways

As a holiday area, the western coastal strip of Clwyd was littered with 'toy' or miniature railways, offering holidaymakers short trips on little trains for a few pence. The largest of these miniature railways was at Rhyl, where a line ran around the Marine Lake (behind the Pleasure Beach funfair). This little railway still exists, despite many troubles in recent years, and can be seen on the left side of the main line from Holyhead, as Chester-bound trains approach Rhyl station. There were a few other 'toy' railways in the county, although they are no longer in existence.

Between Chirk and Glyn Ceiriog once ran the Glyn Valley Tramway, a steam-operated narrow-gauge line built to serve a local quarry, which also operated a passenger service. Sadly, like much of the main-line network, it no longer exists.

The 'Central Station' on Rhyl's Marine Lake in the 1920s, with two of the Marine Lake miniature railway trains preparing to depart watched by a large crowd. The miniature railway lines at the Marine Lake were laid in March 1911, and the little trains could accommodate sixty-four passengers, the fare being 1s. (5p) for adults and 6d. (2½p) for children.

The Miniature Railway, Marine Lake and Park, Rhyl.
omotive built by Messrs. BASSETT-LOWKE, LTD., LONDON & NORTHAMPTON.

One of the locos and its train at the Rhyl Miniature Railway station shortly after opening. The locos used on the railway were all built by Bassett-Lowke, which was famous as builders of miniature engines and was even involved in the Lakeside and Haverthwaite Railway in the Lake District.

Outside the locoshed of the Rhyl Miniature Railway. The four locos are like miniature versions of their sisters operating on the Great Central Railway.

A full train runs past the Miniature Railway's locoshed as a driver prepares a loco for the day's work. The lease for the land on which the railway ran was owned by Rhyl Amusements Ltd, and was terminated in 1969.

A train runs round the Marine Lake watched by summer visitors.

Another train full of passengers has just departed from the station. In the background is the funfair at the Pleasure Beach.

A 2–4–2 tender engine built by Bassett-Lowke heads a train round the lake.

The World's Finest Model Railway. Marine Lake, Rhyl
Inspector, CHARLES WATERFIELD.
Who Enlisted in Great War after 50 years on the Stage

The driver of the 2–4–2 poses with railway inspector Charles Waterfield, who is said to have enlisted in the First World War at sixty-six, giving his age as forty-three.

A Rhyl Miniature Railway train is seen by the lake, with the Marine Lake Pleasure Park in the background.

A Bassett-Lowke 2–4–2 loco heads a train full of holidaymakers round the lake.

A 4–4–2 loco, looking very much like a Great Central Railway 'Director' class, at the head of a train close to the amusement park.

The railway's 2–4–2 loco at the head of a train running round the lake. After closure of the miniature railway, following expiry of the lease, one of the locos was displayed at the main-line station in Rhyl. One was eventually displayed at the Birmingham Railway Museum, Tyseley.

Colwyn Bay also had its own miniature railway, running at the bottom of the embankment which carries the main Chester and Holyhead line through the town. Here in this 1950s view, Pacific locomotive *Prince Charles* is at the head of one of these trains. As late as the mid-1970s, some of the old track was still *in situ*.

Gwrch Castle Railway and station, with American-style loco *Belle of New York* at the head of a full train. The railway owner is standing on the running plate of the loco, watched by a number of visitors. After closure, the line is reputed to have been attacked by vandals.

The Glyn Valley Tramway was a narrow-gauge line built to carry slate from a nearby quarry, and ran between Chirk and Glyn Ceiriog. The line was eventually used for passenger services and one of the trains is seen at Glyn Ceiriog station early this century. The train is hauled by *Sir Theodore*.

CHIRK AND GLYNCEIRIOG (Week Days only.)
(GLYN VALLEY TRAMWAY)

		a.m.		p.m.		p.m.	p.m.
Chirk	dep	10 0		1 40		3 35	6 5
Pontfaen	,,	R		R		R	R
Castle Mill	,,	10 11		1 51		3 45	6 14
Pontfadog	,,	10 23		2 3		3 58	6 26
Dolywern	,,	10 31		2 11		4 6	6 34
Glynceiriog	arr	10 40		2 20		4 15	6 43

		a.m.	a.m. K	noon	p.m. S	p.m.	p.m.
Glynceiriog	dep	7 40	11 0	12 0	2 25	4 40	6 50
Dolywern	,,	7 49	11 9	12 9	2 34	4 49	6 57
Pontfadog	,,	7 57	11 17	12 17	2 41	4 57	7 5
Castle Mill	,,	8 9	11 29	12 29	2 51	5 9	7 15
Pontfaen	,,	R	R	R	R	R	R
Chirk	arr	8 20	11 40	12 40	3 0	5 20	7 25

K—Wednesdays only.   R—Calls to pick up or set down Passengers.   S—Saturdays only.

A timetable for services along the Glyn Valley Tramway.

Acknowledgements

Thanks go to those who supplied photographs used in this work, including Lens of Sutton, Roger Carpenter, Bruce Ellis, Gwyn and Brenda Roberts. We are also grateful to Peter Owen for allowing us to raid his collection of photographs, railway ephemera and timetables, which have proved very useful. Finally, special thanks to Alwen and Gary, without whose support preparation of this book would have been much more difficult.